Two Become One

God's Blueprint for Couples

Donald M. Joy & Robbie B. Joy

Two Become One

God's Blueprint for Couples

Donald M. Joy & Robbie B. Joy

**Evangel
Publishing House**

Nappanee, Indiana 46550

Toll-Free Order Line: (800) 253-9315
Internet Website: www.evangelpublishing.com

Cover Photo © Digital Vision
Edited by Joseph D. Allison and Dimples Kellogg

Publisher's Cataloging-in-Publication Data

Joy, Donald M. (Donald Marvin), 1928–
    Two become one : God's blueprint for couples / Donald M. Joy & Robbie Joy. — 1st ed.
    p. cm.
    Includes bibliographical references and index.
    LCCN 2001099475
    ISBN 1-928915-27-2

    1. Marriage—Religious aspects—Christianity.
I. Joy, Robbie B., 1929– II. Title.

BV4596.M3J69 2002   248.4
                         QBI02-200402

Printed in the United States of America

02 03 04 05 06 07 / 10 9 8 7 6 5 4 3 2 1

Table of Contents

Dedication

for the many who have joined us in the
journey between Eden and the Marriage Supper of the Lamb
and who have trusted us as guides
toward that goal of achieving
"Two Become One"

Foreword

We first met Don and Robbie Joy at an Italian bistro on a pristine day in Seattle more than a decade ago. But we knew them long before that by reputation. And what a reputation they have! They are some of the most transparent, thought-provoking, and grounded biblical teachers on relationships we know. If you've had the privilege of reading one of their previous books, you know what we mean. And if you are new to their work, you are in for a treat.

In *Two Become One*, Don and Robbie tackle some of the thorniest issues surrounding marriage, and they do so with finesse and grace. They have a way of unpacking otherwise confusing and often mangled theological constructs and revealing God's truth within them. But they don't stop there. The Joys then show us in practical terms how to apply that truth to our relationships. This is not a heady book for intellectuals, though it will certainly get you thinking. It is a book for every serious student of God's Word who wants to better live the life God calls us to—as husband and wife.

Whether you have been married only a short while or for decades, this book's message will hit you where you live. Maybe you are engaged or "on the edge of commitment." You'll want to read this book as well. Read it as a couple or study it in a small group. A book like this is not meant to be checked off your reading "to-do" list. It is meant to be read and reread, studied and savored. Read it for all it's worth and your relationship with each other, and with God, will never be the same.

You can look at other books in the myriad of marriage material on the market and be hard-pressed to find many that come up to the biblical and practical standards of *Two Become One*. Frankly, we don't know of another resource quite like it. And since we make it our business to read most marriage books that come out, we should know.

Don and Robbie are living lessons in the message of this book. They not only walk the walk, they carry a lantern that sheds a light on the entire process for those of us who are willing to journey with them. And what a privilege it is.

Drs. Les and Leslie Parrott
Seattle Pacific University

Introduction

If you could have watched the closing ceremony at the Joy breakfast table in the first seventeen years of my life, you would have seen Dad reaching for his well-worn KJV Bible resting on the deck of the china cabinet. Inserted in that Bible was a Sunday school quarterly left open to next Sunday's opening page of the lesson. Turning back to all of us at the table, Dad would consult the fine print below the title to identify today's brief Scripture reading. He would locate that passage in the Bible, read it, then reinsert the quarterly in that location in the Bible, and return the Bible to the china cabinet.

We would then fall to our knees at our chairs and pray. Dad or Mother would open the prayer, then each of us kids would pray in birth order— three of us. When the last voice went silent we began the cadence of the Lord's Prayer (using the "debts" version), closed with "Amen," and were on our feet immediately. On school days, there was sometimes a visible rush because the bus driver was often in the front yard honking the horn, trying to get the delinquent three off our knees to board his bus.

Those mornings listening to Scripture and falling on our knees blur into one solid memory of our family's priorities during those decades. Only one repeating memory of content sticks in my mind. Much too often, it seems in retrospect, Dad would announce the Scripture passage and begin to read with a wide smile on his face. He was delighted (too pleased it seems now) to return to a passage beginning with Ephesians 5:22. In the old King James Version, it said:

> Wives, submit yourselves unto your own husbands, as unto the Lord. For the husband is the head of the wife, even as Christ is the head of the church: and he is the saviour of the body. Therefore as the church is subject unto Christ, so *let* the wives *be* to their own husbands in every thing.

The three of us would see Dad's grin and then would turn to look at Mother. She would typically smile right back at him and let him read on.

Wives Submitting to Husbands

At that breakfast table, we knew that Dad and Mother were not adversaries, and we knew that any demand that one of them do all of the submitting was ridiculous. Instead we experienced our parents in that amazing paradox of "two as one." The generations have rolled forward by more than sixty years and I now know that the old King James Version was careful about many things, but careless about the key word in this passage. Notice above that the words *let* and *be* are in italics. We learned early that the translators supplied such words in italics when they were not actually in the Greek text. Remarkably, they failed to italicize *submit yourselves*, yet the word for "submit" is only in Ephesians 5:21—the previous verse. It looks suspicious that the International Uniform Sunday School Committee consistently and knowingly failed to include verse 21: "Submitting yourselves one to another in the fear of God."

Better yet, the Committee could have begun with 5:15 or 5:18—either of which grounds submission in the context of being wise or being filled with the Spirit. What follows in 5:19–21 are three gerunds denoting the effects of being filled with the Spirit:

> Speaking to yourselves in psalms and hymns . . .
> Giving thanks always for all things . . .
> Submitting yourselves one to another . . .

The only culture in which women uniformly submit to men and where men control women is the culture of evil—of sin.

"He Shall Rule Over You"

In this book, we will explore every Scripture text that might throw light on how the mystery of "two become one" interfaces with the persisting demand for men to control women and for women to "graciously submit to their servant husbands." We will also explore the controlling myth that "man is incomplete" and that "woman was created to fix the mistake."

As we lay out the story of our love and our frustration, we will document how we were shaped by the wrongheaded teachings of men's control of women and of women's passive submission to men. And we will own our personal central tendencies to fall into the patterns common to all sons of Adam and daughters of Eve.

How to Read This Book

There is no wrong way to read this book. Let your questions guide you. The chapter titles will be a shopping list to take you directly to an issue about which you are curious or troubled. The index at the end of the book is a good place to look up specific terms or even a specific Scripture. You can then go into the chapter that shows the largest block of pages devoted to your curiosity or problem point. Robbie and I would invite you to begin with this Introduction and to take a leisurely tour straight through. But one piece of advice we give you: If you are offended by the questions we raise or the guidance we offer, lay the book aside. Keep it close so that when your relationship or your marriage begins to bother you, you can pick it up again. All relationships are in process, and most of us need all the help we can get to find our sense of identity and our way of relating to one another.

Donald and Robbie Joy
600 North Lexington Avenue
Wilmore, KY 40390
859-858-3817
rodojoy@juno.com
www.geocities.com/donaldmjoy

1

Young Love:
Can This Be Eden?

On Friday, September 13, 1946, the first major social event of the new college year, I called at the women's campus residence for Robbie Bowles. We have been exclusively "going steady" even since.

When I discovered what an amazing woman Robbie was, I knew she was one of a kind. I liked her spunk, her vitality, her contagious social grace, magic, and humor. An introvert myself, I was delighted to be alongside someone who moved through a crowd as if she were made for it.

I was quite sure that my tribal clan would endorse my discovery. So by spring break of 1947, it was time to take her home.

Robbie and I had to go through the entire protocol to arrange for her to visit my parents' home. The plan for this trip had to be filed with the college residence hall authorities and, most important of all, Robbie had to be made ready for the visit. She had done her part. She had taken the bus to Wichita, where her Aunt Sue lived. Together they had bought a new Easter outfit, appropriate for the maiden visit to the Joy homestead.

When Robbie modeled the new clothes for me, I was elated at the smart beauty of the outfit. But I was inwardly distressed. There was a minor violation of a tribal taboo. The dainty straw hat was circled with a delicate ring of silk flowers. Robbie read the pain in my countenance.

"Grandpa will not like that hat," I said lamely.

It was almost too complicated to explain. Grandpa Charles Wesley Joy was consistently a delegate to the West Kansas Annual Conference of the Free Methodist Church. He was a first-generation believer in his family line, following Grandma's faithful religious life and heritage. But Grandpa had become the head spokesman for our religious belief and practice. He had even been elected once as General Conference delegate, and those were the people who wrote the *Book of Discipline*.

My Sunday afternoons at Grandpa and Grandma's house were enriched by theological debates, interpretations, and family stories. Women cleared the kitchen, covered the leftovers from the noon meal, saving them for supper just before evening worship service. But the men gathered in the living room, I on Grandpa's footstool, huddled in ecstatic learning! There I heard him occasionally enumerate what the membership covenant meant when new members promised to "forever lay aside all superfluous ornaments." That included buttons that buttoned nothing, all jewelry (including finger rings of any kind), and artificial flowers, whether on the altar of the church, on a man's lapel, or circled around the brim of a lovely straw hat. The fine print of the book also excluded the wearing of feathers as being unnatural to humans, in however small a cluster, as in a man's hat band: That was "pure superfluous adornment." We were simple lifestyle people before it was in vogue to be that way.[1]

As I contemplated Robbie's first visit to the Joy home, my anxiety lay in the conflict I felt. I wanted Robbie to pass Grandpa's inspection. I suspect he would have ignored the silk flowers, but I couldn't risk it. So with a razor blade, Robbie and I removed the ring of flowers, reducing the hat to an elegant but very plain straw.

And Robbie was more than fully accepted! In fact, as I escorted her among the Joy clan on that Easter weekend in 1945, I virtually lost her to the attention of all of the important male relatives. Grandpa seemed always to be wanting time to tell her more family stories. Dad was in his rarest extroverted good humor. Even my young brother David, at age five, cornered her in our kitchen. He hugged her around the knees and promised, "I love you, Robbie, and if Don doesn't marry you, I will." Frankly, I was glad to get Robbie back to campus where I could have a little time with her. She had passed the tribal criteria test with flying colors. I had chosen well.

In my view then, a man was supposed to choose, win, and groom a suitable wife. I had drunk deeply at the Joy family's fountain of male

---

[1]When Robbie and I were married in 1948, it was without wedding rings. But by 1951, our denominations's rules were altered by another General Conference, and we were recentered on some abiding principles. The barnacles on the Old Boat of Zion were finally scraped off. We bought our first wedding rings in the summer of 1951.

responsibilities. In time, we would discover that I took too much responsibility, but then the traditional tribal roles served both of us well.

The Man's Traditional Role

I was five weeks short of age twenty when we married. Robbie was just short of nineteen. We were highly compatible. Her expectations of me and my assertion of my role with her matched at a surprisingly high degree. I basically regarded my male responsibilities as the following:

1. Find the right woman.

2. Court her and win her heart.

3. Shape her into an acceptable person as defined by my own and my family's values and expectations.

4. Take full responsibility for her safety, support, and general well-being.

5. Control the environment, her vulnerabilities, and her lack of experience and competence by "being there first" and by making decisions to guarantee her safety and to spare her having to choose, make a mistake, and possibly be hurt.

In executing this set of responsibilities, I was fortunate to have gentle and consistent models in the uncles, grandfathers, great-uncles, and great-grandfathers on all sides of my family. Not only so, but it was clear that they were doing what heads of families were obligated to do according to the Bible. I listened at family prayers to the oft-repeated reading from Ephesians, which tattooed into my mind the idea that wives should "submit to husbands," that children should "obey their parents," and that husbands should "love wives." It all seemed satisfying and orderly. The roles and responsibilities were obvious to anyone. I was secure—not arrogant, I hope, but very secure.

Who Is the Head of the House?

However, in all of this amazing, thoroughly Christian and gentle clan, there was an emerging paradox. In several of the tribal homes, there was a poster framed or cast into plaster of Paris. It announced an unarguable truth:

Christ is the head of this house,
the unseen guest at every meal

the silent listener to
every conversation.

So all of us Joy males sat at tables beneath such a motto and had to acknowledge, as we called the family to prayer, that this home has a Head. It is not the man living here. It is Jesus.

Enough. This is how our story begins. At nineteen, I would have declared that Robbie and I had indeed recaptured Eden and found love as God intended it to be.

Today, more than fifty years later, it is clear to me that my ideas about my own identity and that of my wife, Robbie, were both distorted by the Fall. I was a son of Adam. Robbie was a daughter of Eve. We were unwittingly living out a fallen idea of human relationships. We had never noticed that Eve had another name before disobedience scrambled the Creation design for relationships. More of that later.

In our better moments, we thought of each other as "the other self," but our deformed image of marriage set us up for the greatest vulnerability of all: regarding ourselves as objects, not as persons. Perhaps that is the most pervasive and indelible mark of the first sin. Men were turned into workers who sweat to earn a living. Women were turned into babymakers who descend into the pit of torture to deliver their babies, and whose dependency and adoration sustain the husbands' pattern of "rule over" them.

We had been formed in environments where no one had ever taken the trouble to figure out what was going wrong with marriages. We'll trace in this book the path from our first awakening to how wrong we had been in defining "who we were." Here we will retrace our perceptual journey and open doors for you, in case you have wondered whatever happened to your Eden. Join us, if you are ready, and we will connect the path from Creation to Jesus and accompany you in a continuing walk with the Creator.

Questions People Ask

Q. *You surely aren't recommending by your story that teenagers should marry, are you?*

A. We recommend to families, not teens alone, that together they decide some life priorities. Should you find that "age" and "exclusive, lifelong bonding" come in conflict, you will have little trouble respecting an early relationship and closing your eyes on the age factor. Ideally, it would be convenient if our young were so consumed by school, academics, athletics, and vocational dreams that they didn't notice that they wrestle with powerful hungers for adult intimacy and sexual expression. However, we have supported early marriages for members of our extended family, and we notice that where all of the value issues are laid on top of the table, families with high Christian commitment tend to choose earlier marriages than the national averages. And if those marriages could be studied apart from all of the violent, even "forced" marriages, we believe the survival rate would be very high.

Q. *Was there something different going on in your growing-up years that made early marriage more feasible?*

A. Perhaps. It was not hard to get a job in the late 1940s, either as a drop-out or as a graduate from college. Our starting teaching salaries of $2,100 and $2,400 per year in Minneola, Kansas, do not sound like much today, but they provided adequate support to us then. Our impression is this: Times change, but human loving is pretty consistent across the centuries. Both then and now, the critical issue is whether the families are both emotionally and economically supportive of the top priority: the moral and emotional health of their young. When this priority controls everything else, love always finds a way, even in runaway inflationary times or in times of genuine social or political calamity. Nobody said life was going to be easy, affluent, and without sacrifice. Families fail their young, we think, when they put anything else ahead of their commitment to support the integrity of their young brides and grooms.

2

Sovereigns Empowered:
"Let Them Have Dominion"

Robbie and I grew up in a Bible-teaching church. As a young boy, I was pleased to know that, like Adam, I was a male. The English Bible text told me everywhere that Adam was a bachelor in search of his missing rib— his wife. So by the age of five or six, my cousin Rex and I would check each other's ribs, counting them. On our lucky days, we had an uneven number. This could only mean that God was even now making a woman for each of us.

Growing up a girl, Robbie accepted that the man came first, that the man was the designated master. She took comfort in knowing that a man would always think she was special and would take care of her.

It was not until I was past fifty that I began looking carefully at the Creation narratives in Genesis. As I was turning forty, I was summarizing a major research project, writing journal articles. I had set up a teaching experiment in southern Michigan. I measured the effects of teaching in the church and in the home on children of grades four, five, and six. I had randomized the tests to eliminate the sex differences—placing boys and girls in equal distribution in each of four groups. But when the total head count came out very uneven (62 percent of the total sample were girls), I decided to separate the scoring data by gender. The results were stunning. So I began speculating on what was going on with girls in church and with boys at home that accounted for their significantly different scores in those two environments.[1]

I began reading current research on sex differences in my search to understand what I had found in this study. Two major differences between boys and girls showed up: the reproductive systems and the brain organization. I began directing my students to read these research journals. I wrote and spoke publicly about what I was finding. Dr. James Dobson invited me to his radio broadcast microphone to talk about some of these differences in 1983. He called the tape of that broadcast, "Innate Differences Between Males and Females." Nearly twenty years later, "Focus on the Family" continues to air the tape once or twice every year and it ranks number seven among most requested tapes from that program. I put a careful report of my findings in *Bonding: Relationships in the Image of God*, which first appeared in 1985. The chapter there was called "Conception: Differentiating the Adam."[2] I had been driven back to the Creation accounts in Genesis by my research junket in 1980.

In January of 1980, six graduate school students raised questions about human development and sex differences that would refocus my life and work. I had been reading human development research literature since the late 1960s. But until 1980, I had never seriously gone back to look at the Genesis accounts of Creation. In the spring of 1980, I was slugging through citations my students had turned up in their search to identify how physiological development might trigger moral development. It was clear that something critical occurred when pubescence hit both girls and boys; suddenly, the reasoning about moral questions changed. The eminent Swiss epistemologist, Jean Piaget, had been in search of the reason for that phenomenon when he died.

I discovered in my students' research reports that from conception, boys and girls are identical in physiology until the ninth week. Then their chromosomes trigger developmental differences. The original fetal form is female in structure, so the journey for girls is smooth and uncomplicated. But the XY chromosome combination in little boys puts them through two

---

[1] See for example, my research report in *Value Oriented Instruction in the Church and in the Home* (Bloomington: Indiana University, 1969), available from Ann Arbor: University Microfilms. A popular-level report on the research is "Building Children's Beliefs," which appeared in *Christianity Today*, June 19, 1970.

[2] That book has appeared in more than a dozen printings, most recently revised in 1996 and 1999.

major "surgery" periods. The ninth to twelfth weeks sees their internal reproductive system transformed from open vagina and ovary-placed gonads into a penis and external testes. Then, between the sixteen and twenty-sixth weeks, the boy's brain is restructured from the original female organization. There is a massive elimination of neurological cells, and about 25 million fibers were destroyed from the corpus callosum, connecting the brain hemispheres. This bumpy road toward delivery miscarries more than one-third of the XY babies. It takes 160 XY conceptions to get 106 boys delivered.[3]

So the story of man and woman in Genesis revisits every conception. Like the original Adam, every fetus has the potential for both male and female, and differentiation in utero is reminiscent of the original "splitting of the Adam" into either male or female. We have more in common with each other than we have differences.

The Image of God

Humans were created in the "image" or "likeness" of God. The summary in Genesis 5 is striking. Scripture makes clear that "Adam" was "them." Man and woman together formed what the NRSV translates "Humankind." The English words *Man* and *Adam* are translations of the same Hebrew term, and, in Genesis 5, it is clear the term denotes both male and female "in the likeness of God." "This is the list of the descendants of Adam. When God created humankind, he made them in the likeness of God. Male and female he created them and he blessed them and named them 'Humankind' when they were created" (Gen. 5:1–2, NRSV).

Actually, we have two "Gospels of Creation." In the first (Gen. 1), the distinguishing marks of humans are (1) they appear as God's final work on the "sixth day" of Creation, and (2) humans alone are created "in the image of God." All animals, species by species, "after its kind" are created on the sixth day. This logical, linear Creation account is prehistoric, and must have existed in oral tradition long before the invention of writing. The Scriptures' refrain, "the evening and the morning were the day," and other linguistic patterns seem to demonstrate that the whole day-by-day account was composed for easy memorization.

---

[3]For more detail on sexual differentiation, see chapter 5, "Conception: Differentiating the Adam," in *Bonding: Relationships in the Image of God* (Nappanee, Ind: Evangel Publishing House, 1996).

In the second Gospel of Creation (Gen. 2), also prehistoric in form, the account is cast as a story—also for easy memorization. The key players are God and the "Adam," though it is a God-centered drama: the slow-motion creation of a solitary Adam, shaped by "the breath of God," and the surgical splitting of the Adam into Man and Woman. These humans are "God connected" by the breath of life. While we are made of the same "dust" as the animals, only humans are created in the "image of God" and filled with the "breath of life." God is spirit, and He creates us with a capacity for eternity. "The Spirit Himself bears witness with our spirit" (Rom. 8:16). This denotes that only humans have a moral sense, grounded in the "image of God" with its mirrors of righteousness, holiness, and knowledge, as St. Paul observes in his writings.[4] But there is more: By investing the divine "image" in us, God is deputizing humans as caregivers and responsible tenants of the earth, representing the divine Person. While the second Gospel of Creation winds down with human failure, we see no revoking of the challenge to tend and care for the planet. In that Gospel, when things go bad, God benevolently relocates the pair east of Eden, far from the Tree of Life, lest they should eat of it and live forever in their broken condition.[5]

We can rule out the idea that our physical appearance reflects the "image of God" in any way. Deity chose to change form, shape, and appearance when Jesus "became flesh and dwelt among us" (John 1:14). That was an invasion of another order of being for the second person of the Trinity. So both Adam and Jesus were the "image of God" in some way other than physical structure.[6]

When we read in Hebrews 1:3 that Jesus was "the express image" of God, the text signifies that He "became the exact representation of God's being." So we may be on the trail of the core issue about humans' being created in "the image of God." Have we not been made representatives of God on this planet?

For more than thirty years, we have been collecting research on moral reasoning. One of the absolutely baffling things about humans is that every generation is born with an innate sense of both justice and attachment. These findings are nicely documented in the reports of Jean Piaget,

---

[4]See Ephesians 4:24 and Colossians 3:10 for St. Paul's three attributes of the image of God endowed on humans.

[5]Again, see *Bonding* for more commentary on Genesis 1 and 2 and their gracious insights for discovering our human identity today.

[6]Genesis 1:26–31 and Hebrews 1:3.

Lawrence Kohlberg, and Carol Gilligan in Europe and North America.[7] Humans are also innately endowed with a conserving tendency that we can describe only as "innocence." So every child has an instinctual tendency to dream of lifelong exclusive sexual intimacy. When that pattern showed up in the research by Robert Coles of Yale, for example, he confessed his surprise that the children of the "flower children" of the 1960s still expected that their first love would be their only lifelong love.[8] It becomes supremely clear that God has planted original grace and a hunger for righteousness/justice universally in humans. Theologians have been inclined to speak of "original sin" and the "Fall," but theological wisdom also needs to account for the gift of innocence that we see in each wave of newborns. Are we looking at evidence of "original grace" and "aspiration"?

We might think that the "image of God" grants humans godlike possibilities. Indeed, there is a sense in which we have been created "a little lower than God" (Ps. 8:5, NRSV).[9] When we compare the spectrum of God's attributes with human potentials, striking mirror images of God's essence leap out:

1. *God is omniscient,* knowing past, present and future. Humans hold the past in memory, the present in sensory perception, and the future in imagination. So a sense of history and destiny seems to be a uniquely human characteristic among the earth's creatures. Other sixth-day creatures seem to survive by unchanging, blind instinct. Each generation returns to the same breeding grounds to repeat the life agenda that has remained virtually unchanged across centuries. But humans are invested with imagination, which takes us into new environments and inspires ways of adapting to changing circumstances, even within one generation.

2. *God is omnipotent.* Humans accept the charge to "have dominion." Humans are "sovereigns" in God's image. We aspire to self-direction and to creative management of all dimensions of the creation, now including cyberspace!

---

[7]See, for example, the discussion of these research bases in Donald M. Joy, ed., *Moral Development Foundations*, especially chapter one, "Life as Pilgrimage" (Nashville: Abingdon, 1983), reprinted annually in a course text, and available at Cokesbury at Asbury Seminary, Wilmore, KY 40390, as *Moral Development and Ministry.*

[8]Robert Coles and Geoffrey Stokes, *Sex and the American Teenager* (New York: Harper Colophon Books, 1985).

[9]Read Psalm 8.

3. *God is creator*. Humans not only reproduce new humans "in the image of God" (sometimes to our surprise), but also are magnificently creative and resourceful. Music, poetry, novels—all forms of art—invariably echo the creativity of God. All creativity derives from God's capital and gift, whether the art is holy or obscene. God's "image" is a free and unrestricted gift. So when we drive to Bardstown, Kentucky, to see *The Stephen Foster Story*, we revel in the magnificent and simple beauty of young Stephen Foster's music and we celebrate the faithfulness of God's gifts of creativity. But we come home in grief that Foster's talent was so scarcely treasured and so quickly wasted by an ironic combination of poor choices, bad company, and dependency on alcohol. A similar pathos emerges in the movie *Amadeus*, which chronicles the uncommon gifts of Wolfgang Amadeus Mozart—early wasted by the self-destructive forces that dogged his brief lifetime.

God has so invested the divine image in our humanity that we are inescapably God's representatives. We are spontaneously moral or immoral, but (unlike other warm-blooded creatures) we are never amoral. Fathers and mothers spontaneously carry out a thousand operations in behalf of their children, but so do all the rest of us. We are created to relate to other people, to comfort the grieving, to rescue the dying, and to reach out to the lonely and the sick. All of that is "imaging God." And if we choose to save ourselves to withdraw from the impulses to help, to rescue, and to touch, then we are denying the image of God within us.

Sovereignty to Humans

Genesis 1 describes the mystery of humans created in the image of God, and assigns God's characteristic of sovereignty to them:

> [26]Then God said, "Let us make humankind in our image, according to our likeness; and let them have dominion over the fish of the sea, and over the birds of the air, and over the cattle, and over all the wild animals of the earth, and over every creeping thing that creeps upon the earth."

> [27]So God created humankind in his image,
>   In the image of God he created them;
>   Male and female he created them.
> [28]God blessed them, and God said to them, "Be fruitful and multiply, and fill the earth and subdue it; and have dominion

over the fish of the sea and over the birds of the air and over every living thing that moves upon the earth." (vv. 26–28, NRSV)

Notice that Genesis 1 says that both the male and the female were created "in the image of God," as the pronoun *them* indicates. And notice that the God who creates has a plural identity: He says, "Let us" create humans "in our image" and in "our likeness." This clear mark of community in the nature of God suggests Trinity, and it sets the scene for the second Gospel of Creation to note, "Then the LORD God said, 'It is not good that the man should be alone; I will make him a helper as his partner'" (Gen. 2:18, NRSV).[10]

The identity of Adam is put in perspective in Genesis 5:1–2, returning to the first Creation Gospel's way of naming by God. "They" are *Adam*, here translated "Humankind." For consistency, the word *Adam* should always be translated "humankind": "This is the list of the descendants of Adam. When God created humankind, he made them in the likeness of God. Male and female he created them, and he blessed them and named them 'Humankind' when they were created" (vv. 1–2, NRSV). The evidence is clear: "They" were created "in the image of God," and "they" were given dominion over the world, but never over each other.

Jesus once told a story about a certain steward who was empowered by a landowner to take full responsibility for the land and its care. Then the landowner left the scene (Matt. 25:14–30). The story is remarkably focused on human empowerment and human responsibility to God. It emphasizes that we are created in God's image.

On another occasion, Jesus was questioned on the point of whether taxes were due to Caesar:

> [17]"Tell us, then, what you think. Is it lawful to pay taxes to the emperor, or not?" [18]But Jesus, aware of their malice, said, "Why are you putting me to the test, you hypocrites? [19]Show me the coin used for the tax." And they brought him a denarius. [20]Then he said to them, "Whose head is this, and whose title?" [21]They answered, "The emperor's." Then he said to them, "Give therefore to the emperor the things that are the emperor's, and to God the things that are God's." (Matt. 22:17–21, NRSV)

---

[10]Literally, "a companion corresponding to" (NASB note).

The emperor's money with his "head" or picture on it becomes a parable about the coinage of God's making: If we embrace the gift of our humanity, the "image" demonstrates that we have obligations to our Maker. So human sovereignty is under God's sovereign accountability.

Splitting the Adam—Into *Ish* and *Ishshah*

The "image of God" gift, announced in the first Gospel of Creation (Gen. 1), has a counterpart in the second Gospel of Creation (Gen. 2). Here, the solitary human, the "Adam," is not "man" in any male or masculine sense. Rather, "Adam" is the "humankind" prototype. Remember that the Hebrew word *Adam* is more accurately translated in the NRSV as "humankind" in Genesis 5, cited above. And all previous uses of "man" in Genesis are actually translations of *Adam*, and hence need to be read as "humankind" to keep us from attributing gender before the sexual differentiation that follows quickly here.

The counterpart to the "image of God" in Genesis 1 is the "breath of God," which gives defining character to the human among the other sixth-day creatures: "then the LORD God formed man from the dust of the ground, and breathed into his nostrils the breath of life; and the man became a living being (Gen. 2:7, NRSV).

The first human is "dust" (*adamah* or literally, "particles"). But once the "breath of life" goes in, the human becomes a "living creature" (*nephesh*). The domestic animals mentioned later in Genesis 2 are also called *nephesh*. So the amazing picture is of a fully sensed, hungry, breathing "temple of the Holy Spirit." The human was created for intimate connection with God. So this first-stage human, completely and wonderfully created and filled with God's breath, is given a first challenge: "The LORD God took the man and put him in the garden of Eden to till it and keep it. And the LORD God commanded the man, 'You may freely eat of every tree of the garden; but of the tree of the knowledge of good and evil you shall not eat, for in the day that you eat of it you shall die'" (Gen. 2:15–17, NRSV).

Once the Adam is morally charged and placed in a servant relationship to God, the next step in the human creation occurs. Notice that God did not say, "Oops! I goofed! I created only half a species!" This was not a heavenly correction of a defective model; this was God's resolve to complete the mystery of the Trinity community in the human species: "Then the LORD God said, 'It is not good that the man [*ha-adam*] should be alone; I will make him a helper as his partner'" (Gen. 2:18, NRSV).

"It is not good"[11] that the Adam should be alone. There is no hint that the need for reproduction was the problem. Indeed, we know of more than 2,000 species that reproduce themselves asexually. But the final touch of God's image required "community." So the search takes an unusual turn; none of the animals can complete this "community" the Adam needs.

The Adam needs a "partner corresponding to the self." The Hebrew language of Genesis 2 suggests a "mirror image" of the self—an "other self," not an inferior "helper"—to meet his need. The NRSV attempts to express this "corresponding" idea with its "helper as his partner" phrase.

> [19]So out of the ground the LORD God formed every animal of the field and every bird of the air, and brought them to the man to see what he would call them; and whatever the man called every living creature, that was its name. [20]The man [ha-adam] gave names to all cattle, and to the birds of the air, and to every animal of the field; but for the man [ha-adam] there was not found a helper as his partner [literally, a companion corresponding to ha-adam]. (Gen. 2:19–20)

God does not establish community between the Adam and animals. Some scholars note that a more shocking teaching may lie here. Bestiality—humans resorting to sexual contact with animals—is forever forbidden by this account. The boundaries are set. The naming of the animals denotes a distinction between the namer and the named. We will be haunted in Genesis 3 to watch the man "name" the woman, and we struggle to this day with the boundary that act put in place between Man and Woman. "So the LORD God caused a deep sleep to fall upon the man [ha-adam], and he slept; then he took one of his ribs and closed up its place with flesh. And the rib that the Lord God had taken from the man he made into a woman [Ishshah] and brought her to the man" (Gen. 2: 21–22, NRSV).

I refer to this surgery as the "original splitting of the Adam." No new material, not even additional "dust particles/atoms," were added. So this is sexual differentiation. When every baby is conceived, it first develops everything necessary to become either male or female; but that differentiation comes only in the ninth to the twelfth weeks of gestation. It

---

[11]Compare this to Genesis 1, where "very good" is the designation of the male-female creation in the Trinity community image: "Let us, create the Adam in our image and in our likeness."

is such a risk to turn the essentially "female" fetus into a male that there are more than 50 miscarriages of males to get 106 males born. We lose the high number of XY chromosome boys because of the trauma and potential errors when the testicles drop from the ovary position and are enclosed in a scrotum formed from the vaginal lips, while the clitoris is refitted as a penis. The bright scar that runs full circle from the anus around the scrotum and up the base of the penis of a boy is the differentiation scar. It may be a reminder of the Creation scar that seems to extend the full length of the torso. But it was obviously worth it, and the second Gospel of Creation fairly sings with the ecstasy of the new community as male and female:

> [23]Then the man said,
> "This at last is bone of my bones
>   And flesh of my flesh;
> this one shall be called Woman [*Ishshah*],
>   For out of Man [*Ish*] this one was taken."
> [24]Therefore a man [*Ish*] leaves his father and his mother and
> clings to his wife [Ishshah], and they become one flesh. [25]And
> the man and his wife were both naked, and were not ashamed.
> (Gen. 2:23–25, NRSV).

The individuals' Hebrew names are not Adam and Eve; they are *Ish* and *Ishshah*. More of that renaming later. *Woman* is first used in verse 22, where the article should have been omitted; she is Woman, not just "a woman." Most Bible translations denote the *Ishshah* as Woman and *Ish* as Man, always capitalized. These were their names fresh from the hand of God, who lives in Trinity community and takes specific care to create community for humans.[12]

In this chapter, we have revisited the Creation as reported in Genesis 1–2. There it is clear that humans, male and female, were created in the image of God, and that God chose to mark them together with the first characteristic of God's nature: sovereignty. We will see that the tragic failure reported in Genesis 3 brings the effects of sin into this relationship, which persistently

---

[12]See my extended treatment of this second Gospel of Creation and sexual differentiation in my *Bonding: Relationships in the Image of God*, Chapter 5, "Conception: Differentiating the Adam."

distort that mutual gift of sovereignty represented in God's declaration: "Let *them* have dominion."

Questions People Ask

Q. *I have always thought that Adam was created a bachelor, a full-grown adult male. Are you asking me to think of Adam as some sort of sexual deformity—both male and female?*

A. I am inviting you to look at Genesis 1 and Genesis 2 and to decide what each text says, remembering that they are our two "Gospels of Creation." Genesis 1:27 states simply that "God created humankind [*adam*] in his image, in the image of God he created them…" (NRSV). But Genesis 2, the second Gospel of Creation, tells the same truth in a story format and describes God's creation of a solitary Adam, intimately shaped and finally "in-breathed" with God's Holy Spirit (Gen. 2:7). This human is placed in the Garden of Eden to manage it and its animal population. During that apprenticeship among the animals, as the Adam names them, God announces, "It is not good that the Adam should be alone; I will make him a companion corresponding to the Adam."

So in this story-narrative Gospel of Creation the Storyteller deliberately stresses the deep hunger that all humans have for intimate community. Our clue about the Adam comes from the detail about where Woman [*Ishshah*] came from—completely and exclusively right out of the Adam's body. The theological reason for the "splitting of the Adam" is that it is "not good" for a human being to be alone. There is not the slightest suggestion that God neglected to think through the need for sexual reproduction or for two sexes. The plot line is carefully laid out to stress our need for intimate "community" like that of the Holy Trinity, where two become one (Gen. 2:24) with potential for a Trinity completion. The mystery of "couple" is added to male and female.

Q. *I thought that women were to submit to men. Are you saying that St. Paul was wrong in demanding women's submission? Can a woman obey the Bible and not submit to her husband?*

A. Both men and women were created as sovereigns—to "have dominion" as co-regents in the world. That mystery is patterned after the mystery of the Holy Trinity: "Let us make humankind [the adam] in our image, according to our likeness; and let them have dominion…" (Gen. 1:26, NRSV). Only two sovereigns can "submit to one another out of reverence for Christ," as St. Paul demands (Eph. 5:21, NIV).

In the story "Sir Gawain and the Black Knight," the plot revolves around King Arthur's search for the answer to a question posed by the Black Knight. The Black Knight has challenged Arthur to return a year and a day from today, to risk his life in mortal combat, unless he can answer the question, "What is it that every woman desires most?"

Arthur eventually finds a woman who had been so badly abused that her deformed countenance can be restored only if she finds a good man who truly loves her. She agrees to reveal the answer to the Black Knight's questions only on her wedding day as she marries the king's nephew, Sir Gawain. There she tells Arthur, "What every woman desires most is her sovereignty."

The Black Knight, upon hearing King Arthur's answer, is enraged. "My sister! You have found my sister and she has betrayed me!" he screams, as he whirls and rides away. That story, rooted in oral tradition that may go back to the seventh century, exists in written literature from about the thirteenth century. It testifies to the importance of maintaining inner sovereignty and holy boundaries, thus being able to present a sovereign self, both to public service and to an exclusive and intimate marriage. Nothing less provides a basis for the mystery of "two become one."

We will explore the submission issue from St. Paul in Chapters 6 and 7. It is enough here to note that the verb translated "submit" or "be subject" in Ephesians 5:22 shows up in italics in careful editions of Scripture. This means the *submission* word is missing in the verse that speaks of women. However, it does appear in Ephesians 5:21, the previous verse, where it cuts both ways: "Submit to one another out of reverence for Christ."

If you are a woman, you could ask your husband to join you in asking the question: Can a husband refuse to submit to his wife and be a Bible-believing man? Mutual sovereignty and mutual submission are the happy call on all of us.

3

"Two Become One": The Mystery of Trinity, Intimacy, and Family

Our firstborn arrived on December 12, just before Christmans, and the photographs we cherish from those days capture the wonder on our young faces as we held that special child. We sensed then that he was an extension of each of us. We knew that genetically it was true, even though we still do not begin to understand how a baby gathers generations of traits from two fresh family lines. And we had no idea why it was such a spiritually charged event. But Jurgen Moltmann has cited early Christian teaching that throws light on those feelings we experienced.

According to Moltmann, Gregory of Nazianzus offered a model of the Holy Trinity to clear the minds of Christian believers in the third century. In one of his sermons, Gregory suggested that if anyone has a problem understanding the mystery of the Trinity, one should "look at your breakfast table." There one would see a father, a mother, and a child. They are one, but they are also distinctly three persons. So every family is in the image of the Trinity. Gregory offered Adam, Eve, and Seth as the prototype of a "trinitarian family," the first after tragedy had emptied the first couple's home of the two firstborn sons. A second Gregory sermon addressed how husbands and wives and children regard each other. He reasoned that it is a mirror image of the teaching about the Trinity. Consider that the Holy Trinity resides in community, that they are one. Likewise, the Christian home is marked by this sort of

Trinity-like solidarity. Most of us have acquired a Westernized view of God and the Trinity.[1]

The Trinity as Community

In Genesis 1, God announces, "Let *us* create the human in *Our* image and *Our* likeness . . . Let *them* have dominion . . ." (paraphrase). Jesus' concluding prayer that the Christian believers be "one, as You, Father, are in me and I am in you" (John 17:21, NRSV), stresses how the Trinity mark is still on humans when they rise to their complete destiny. God's statement in Genesis 2, that "It is not good that the human should be alone," also has the sound of community ringing through it.

What makes God the Creator almighty is not some display of archetypal power and punitive force; God is almighty because of persistent, passionate commitment to the whole Creation. God is love, lovingkindness, and righteousness—that is the nature of the divine almightiness. Indeed, in the remarkable exchange between the Lord and Abraham, when Abraham begs

---

[1]See Jurgen Moltmann, *The Trinity and the Kingdom: The Doctrine of God* (New York: Harper and Row, 1981), pp. 194–195. The foundational ideas of this thesis are nicely developed in his Chapter 6, "The Kingdom of Freedom," condensed particularly in the section "Criticism of political and clerical monotheism," pp. 190ff. Moltmann says that the Cappadocian Fathers and Orthodox theologians, to this day, stress "community." Not only do they focus on community, they criticize the modalistic tendencies in the "personal" Trinitarian doctrine of the Western church (p. 199). Moltmann's presentation of the Caesars' reasoning explains how Christianity was chosen to serve the political agendas of the monarchy:

"The polytheism of the heathen is idolatry. The multiplicity of the nations which is bound up with polytheism, because polytheism is its justification, is the reason for the continuing unrest in the world. Christian monotheism is in a position to overcome heathen polytheism. Belief in the one God brings peace, so to speak, in the diverse and competitive world of the gods. Consequently Christendom is the one universal religion of peace. In place of the many cults it puts belief in the one God. What political order corresponds to this faith in one God and the organization of this worship by the one church? It is the Emperor Augustus's kingdom of peace, seen as Rome's enduring obligation and commitment, and as the common hope of the nations" (pp. 194–195).

Moltmann's central point is that Christianity in the Western world was profoundly influenced by the conception of political power and the structure of the monarchy. This monarchial influence, he holds, has verticalized our conception of the Trinity and of all social order whether religious, political, or industrial. So "vertical" was the union between Christianity and the Roman and, later, other European emperors that the absolute unilateral power was attributed to the emperors quite apart from whether they honored God personally or by their arbitrary decisions. They were thus able to live in passive obedience to the vertical monarchy that governed their temporal lives even to execution by the whim of a caesar, a kaiser, or a king. See also L. Hodgson, *The Doctrine of the Trinity* (New York: Charles Scribner's Sons, 1944), p. 95; cf. also A. M. Allchin, *Trinity and Incarnation in Anglican Tradition* (London: Oxford University Press, 1977); cf. also Geervarghese Mar Osthathios, *Theology of a Classless Society* (London: 1979), pp. 147 ff.

for the city of Sodom to be spared, an ancient text leaves a clue that it was God who "remained standing before Abraham," pleading for the city when Abraham had given up. But some modern Bible expositors seem to have altered the narrative to match their perceptions of a punitive God, who in cold and monarchial decree determined to destroy the city.[2]

The glorious power of God, the Father, Son, and Holy Spirit does not show itself by seizing power from other competing forces. Instead, the amazing, life-giving power of the Trinity consistently rises out of weakness. God's power is revealed not, as Elijah discovered, in the wind, the earthquake, or the fire, but in the "still small voice" or "a gentle whisper."[3] Jesus confirms this in His surrender to His Father's will, even though that required His death.

Repeatedly, the power of God is expressed by collecting communities that appear to be fragile and weak. Those communities are consistently showing affection, trust, and order. The witness of God's power in the world is lived out through those communities, always imperfectly, but nevertheless powerfully.

The great "humiliation of God"—namely, His downward transformation into the incarnation of God in Jesus—is taken to its ultimate when Jesus is shamefully murdered. But a further risk of God has the Holy Spirit investing the work of the Son in the unlikely apostles, as they are empowered to take the gospel to the whole world. So the creating, redeeming, empowering God works through fragile, unlikely instruments to call a broken and imperfect world to bring its brokenness and its weakness to the new community of faith.

We cite these teachings about the Trinity to suggest that community, not power, is the overall priority for God whose activities we trace to the work of Father, Son, and Holy Spirit. But we also cite them to open a window on a central characteristic of God: complete devotion to relationships without undue concern for hierarchical structures, roles, or status.

The Trinity as Family?

In our human hierarchical way of seeing all relationships, we have had a tendency to see God on the top, Jesus in the middle, and the Holy Spirit at

---

[2]See Genesis 18:22, especially the footnote in the New International Version that reads, "Masoretic text, an ancient scribal tradition *"but the Lord remained standing before Abraham."*

[3]See 1 Kings 19:11–13.

the bottom, dangling in connection to both Father and Son. All of this reflects the politics of kings, presidents, and CEOs. These images have become part of the air we breathe in our political and ecclesial environments. Like fish, unaware of their environment of water, we rarely contemplate the ideas immersing us. No fish will ever write a book about water until it is flung on dry land and becomes aware of its total dependence on water.

Our hierarchical language about God has come to us out of Greek philosophy more than from Scripture. Greek idealistic philosophy gave us the language of omnipotence, omniscience, and omnipresence to describe the transcendental world of mind and spirit that the Greeks held to be superior to our own lesser world of "matter." As Christianity spread through the early centuries, Christian teachers tried to describe God's knowledge by dipping into the Greek vocabulary of "omniscience." Soon they borrowed phrases to describe the other "attributes" of God from Plato's idealistic philosophy. The roots of this verticalizing of the Trinity can be found as early as the second century. Christian thinkers were trying to communicate with the Greco-Roman culture; so from the fourth century on, Plato's concepts were borrowed to express Christian concepts. Much later, as the Middle Ages ended, Aristotle's system of logic was integrated into Christian theology, and the shift from biblical categories to a Greco-Roman imperial and philosophical model was complete.

But contemplate the biblical accounts: God, Jesus, and the Holy Spirit are represented in Scripture as "coming near" to us. They themselves are depicted as living in community. Both the pre-Roman church and the continuing Eastern church have a community view of the Trinity, not a monarchial one. Those traditions hold that marriage is a "nuptial community" modeled on the Holy Trinity.[4] Bride, groom, and "couple"

---

[4]See Clifford Stevens, "The Trinitarian Roots of the Nuptial Community," *St. Vladimir's Theological Quarterly, Journal* 35, no. 4 (1991): 351–358. Stevens notes, "It is a well-known fact that East and West have vastly different traditions of marriage and that the Western tradition tends to reflect the Neo-Platonist and Stoic reservations about matter, the body, and the senses. Except for certain exaggerated statements in Origen, St. Gregory of Nyssa and certain early monastic writers, the East rejected the dualism of Neo-Platonist anthropology, even though it found in Neo-Platonist thought a rich vocabulary for the expression of religious and mystical truths. While accepting some of its vocabulary, the East rejected as contrary to revelation the anthropological dualism of Origen and Evagrius Ponticus and refused to accept an anthropology that despised the senses, fashioning instead a theory of the philanthropy of God, which saw in the sense life of human beings the generosity of the Godhead, making accessible to human experience the beneficence of an inaccessible God. This radical difference between East and West

denote the mystery of the "two become one." Father, mother, and child—as Gregory of Nazianzus reminds us from so long ago—are also in the image of the Holy Trinity: The child proceeds form the father and from the mother, just as the Holy Spirit proceeds from the Father and from the Son.

What a recovery of the marriage and family metaphors of the Holy Trinity might do for us is staggering to the imagination. It would illuminate the sense of how the "image of God" is visible in the world. It would send us seeking out the lonely, orphans, and widows in their abandonment, in order to bring them into a significant Trinitarian community of care and support. It would rebuke the disease of privatism that plagues most of the Western world. It might take off the fear that holds so many young adults away from making a commitment and embracing responsibility for a home and a family.

Rome: A Vertical Trinity?

It is easy to recognize how Western ideas about an imperial pope, modeled on Caesar, required that a celibate priest rule a world church. All of this flies in the face of a balanced view of the Trinity as a mystery best represented by relationships experienced in the family. Ironically, even the hierarchy of the Roman Catholic Church uses family titles: "Pope" literally means "Papa" or "Daddy," and the celibate priest is universally given the title of "Father." But the papal pageantry, costuming, and traditional role are those of Caesar—the imperial ruler of a world empire.

Lest you take too much pleasure in painting the pope in imperial colors, take a close look at the behavior of your own clergy. Dictatorships, let us admit, may be seen in many church locations. Many Christians need not travel to Rome to find a pope. They may be kissing the imperial ring of a tyrant every Sunday. When one of my classes toured a superchurch operation, one student asked the senior minister, "Can you describe your finance committee?" His instant response: "You're looking at it."

Many of us may find it difficult to stop seeing the Trinity in a vertical hierarchy, with imperial overtones attributed to the Sovereign One. But all of us should contemplate the possibility that our experience of God and the

---

is seen most especially in the Eastern theology of marriage, which has no trace of the anthropological pessimism inherent in Western theology. The East, true to its Patristic heritage, sees man and woman as the icons of God in their sexual reality and recognizes in the nuptial community a reflection of that intimate giving and embracing of the 'other' which is the heart of Trinitarian theology" (excerpt from opening of the journal article). For more Trinitarian implications within this Eastern Orthodox perspective, see also John D. Zizioulas, *Being as Communion* (Crestwood, NJ: St. Vladimir's Seminary Press, 1993).

record of the acts of God in all persons throughout Scripture are illuminated by the marital and family images. Many of the power struggles in the churches, the splitting of denominations, and the general adversary positioning of one Christian group against another "in the name of God" might be greatly reduced if we conceptualized the Trinity in community terms instead of imperial ones.

I once served with a consulting team for the Office of the Chief of Chaplains as a seminar trainer in chapels of the U.S.A.F.E. command. This tour included a few days housed at Izmir, Turkey. I was startled to discover we were in biblical Smyrna. Our training event was canceled on George Washington's birthday because it was an official holiday for U.S. military installations. Our host chaplain quickly ordered up a nine-passenger Chevrolet station wagon, a Turkish driver, and a U.N. Turkish translator, and we set off for a full day's visit to the ancient city of Ephesus, known today as Efes. It sits on the coastline of the Aegean Sea. We were fascinated by the standing remains of the great amphitheater where St. Paul's life was threatened by Diana worshipers. We walked through the remains of the Celsus Library, the baths, and the adjoining *Ask Evi* bedrooms of the women of the night. We saw the ruins of a Christian church planted right across the street from these establishments in the city center. Then we moved to the crest of the prominence overlooking the Aegean Sea. We found the ruins of a mosque constructed within sight of gigantic stones visibly marked with the symbols of an Egyptian fertility goddess. We looked south at a mammoth hole, which our Turkish guide told us was the site of the Temple of Diana, the dominant fertility goddess. Most of it is in the British Museum, he mused. "But you can see the magnificent columns that are integrated into the Haija Sophia in Istanbul."

We turned around and found we were viewing all of this from a great marble floor. It was the vast Church of St. John, its floor a marble slab as large as a ball field. A few of its columns were still standing. They once supported the superstructure and a roof—all now missing. I was intrigued to see (at eye level) crosses wrapped around these marble columns. Dating back to about the year A.D. 100, these crosses featured "clubbed" cross pieces. At the end of each stem of the crosses was a Trinity cluster. I suddenly felt a chill. These Trinity symbols were in use before the church moved to Rome, where the pope's hat resembles the imperial crown. What would the Trinity symbols have looked like if Rome had invented them? The crosses at Ephesus represent each person of the Trinity with a circle. All of the circles are of equal size with no designated order of any kind. Each is interchangeable with the others.

We are always captive to our God images and "act out" our perceptions of God in our moments of highest motivation. Even the relationship between the sexes might be altered toward mutual respect if we saw the collected family at the breakfast table as a reminder of the collegiality of God. The exploitive, imperial sexual adventures of males' using females might give way to a holy kind of intimacy, should we see the intimate community of lovers as God's witness to us of the nature of the Trinity.

"I in Them, as You Are in Me, Let Them Be One in Us!"

The moving prayer of Jesus recorded for us in John 17 evokes intimate images of the Trinity, calling the church and the family to a unity that comes only in community. For nearly twenty years of our teaching together, we have used this "prayer prayed for you," emphasizing two things that leap out of the text:

1. The prayer for becoming "one" assumes the Holy Spirit inhabits the believers as they come together in community. The entire prayer assumes the presence of the Holy Spirit, though only Father and Son are named in this Trinity-focused prayer.

2. The Trinity we see in John 17 is one of intimacy, collegiality, and empowerment of everyone gathered into the Trinity circle. Remarkably, the role of Jesus as "Son" is, in this prayer, in transition. So He prays that His frightened and fragile apostles will be transformed into what will become the body of Christ. Look at Jesus' twice-repeated cry for "becoming one" recorded in John 17:20–23:

> [20]I ask not only on behalf of these, but also on behalf of those who will believe in me through their word, [21]that they may all be one. As you, Father, are in me and I am in you, may they also be in us, so that the world may believe that you have sent me. [22]The glory that you have given me I have given them, so that they may be one, as we are one, [23]I in them and you in me, that they may become completely one, so that the world may know that you have sent me and have loved them even as you have loved me. (NRSV)

Try to grasp a picture of that Father-Son-Believer "oneness." It consists of *Jesus in the Father and the Father in Jesus.* Believers are to have the same reciprocal, mutual, intimate relationship: "that they may be one, as we are one": *Believer A connected to Believers X, Y, and Z.* But the picture focuses on the Trinity: *Believers in Jesus and Father, Jesus in all, Father in Jesus.* The New Testament's intensive teaching on the Holy Spirit who inhabits human agents unfolds in John 14, 15, and 16. Now in Chapter 17, there is no specific mention of the Holy Spirit, but it is clear that the believing disciples are the temples inhabited by the Holy Spirit. This brings the believers right up into intimate fellowship with Father and Son!

In this chapter, we have seen that the family may provide us with direct experiences and metaphors to help us understand God, alongside the formal doctrine of the Trinity. We have looked at the possibility that our images of the Trinity may have been deformed by the medieval political environment, where Christianity was corrupted into a secular power model. To the extent that Christians have "imperialized" the Trinity, we have abandoned intimacy, mutuality, and the high participation of community—not only in our families, but likely in our communities of faith as well.

Questions People Ask

Q. *Where can I go to find a local church that sees the family as the image of the Trinity? I am so eager to follow the Scripture trail you offer here, but I'm not used to hearing about the Trinity, period. And looking at marriage and the family through the lens of the Trinity is far from the kind of teaching I'm hearing.*

A. You are not alone, but some suggest that the twenty-first century will usher in fresh understanding of the Trinity. Combine that prediction with another—that in order to understand people, we must begin to see them in their various "systems." This means observing that any one person is a member of several relational systems: spouse to spouse, parent to family, child to family of origin, employee to professional peers, and so forth. Both of these predictions suggest an awakening to the deep hungers we all have for meaningful relationships.

So in your search, look for a local church where these hungers are high on the priorities of the congregation. There you will likely find leaders who combine a dedication to Scripture with profound compassion for people and their needs. They are most open to identifying God's activity through the Holy Spirit today.

4

"Head of the House" : God's Order for Families?

Robbie and I were guests of a great church in Arlington, Texas, during a spring writing sabbatical while I worked on the first draft of *Bonding*. We volunteered to lead an intergenerational Tuesday night ministry for the church. After one of those sessions, three of the fathers approached me. Would I like to join them for a popular men's Bible study later in the week? They were going every week to Lovers Lane United Methodist Church. They explained the rules: I could go as a guest, but only regulars who completed their homework could participate in the small group Bible-sharing portion. And everyone was simply an "auditor" when the regular teacher taught the whole group. With any luck, they said, I could pick up the Bible study notes written by the founder of the Bible-study program.

It was a half-hour drive to the church and the whole evening went very well. The evening's focus was a survey of the book of Esther. I had read the book with interest, but had never cracked it in depth, as the small groups had been doing for a week of personal study. (It was good to be "silenced" as a visitor. I do my share of talking and leading, but at the bone-marrow level I am an introvert, and I listen well.)

An Exxon executive gave us the clear lecture for the evening. I learned he had been trained in California by the founder of this Bible-study program. This meant that his leader notes were from the official movement script. He lectured from the "epistle lectern" in that gracious divided-chancel sanctuary. As he unpacked the narrative story of the book of Esther, I noticed his smooth delivery hit a bump. He apologized as he announced what now haunts me as one of the "lost chords" of biblical misunderstanding.

"It is a little embarrassing to see the context," he said shifting into this confidential notice, "but we have here in chapter 2 'God's order for families.'"

Notice why the lecturer was embarrassed by the overall narrative in which his key phrase was set: King Ahasuerus was hosting a six-month drinking spree. His queen refused to display herself to his drunken guests, so his cabinet leaders and governors from 127 provinces urged him to craft a policy to avert having the same thing happen when they returned home. Our Exxon executive simply read the text of Esther 1:

> ¹The events here related happened in the days of Ahasuerus, the Ahasuerus who ruled from India to Ethiopia, a hundred and twenty-seven provinces. ²At this time he sat on his royal throne in Susa the capital city. ³In the third year of his reign he gave a banquet for all his officers and his courtiers; and when his army of Persians and Medes, with his nobles and provincial governors, were in attendance, ⁴he displayed the wealth of his kingdom and the pomp and splendour of his majesty for many days, a hundred and eighty in all.

> ⁵When those days were over, the king gave a banquet for all the people present in Susa, the capital city, both high and low; it was held in the garden court of the royal pavilion and lasted seven days. ⁶There were white curtains and violet hangings fastened to silver rings with bands of fine linen and purple; there were alabaster pillars and couches of gold and silver set on a mosaic pavement of malachite and alabaster, of mother-of-pearl and turquoise. ⁷Wine was served in golden cups of various patterns: the king's wine flowed freely as befitted a king, ⁸and the law of the drinking was that there should be no compulsion, for the king had laid it down that all the stewards of his palace should respect each man's wishes. ⁹In addition, Queen Vashti gave a banquet for the women in the royal apartments of King Ahasuerus.

[10]On the seventh day, when he was merry with wine, the king ordered Mehuman, Biztha, Harbona, Bigtha, Abagtha, Zethar, and Carcas, the seven eunuchs who were in attendance on the king's person, [11]to bring Queen Vashti before him wearing her royal crown, in order to display her beauty to the people and the officers; for she was indeed a beautiful woman. [12]But Queen Vashti refused to come in answer to the royal command conveyed by the eunuchs. This greatly incensed the king, and he grew hot with anger.

[13]Then the king conferred with his wise men versed in misdemeanours; for it was his royal custom to consult all who were versed in law and religion, [14]those closest to him being Carshena, Shethar, Admatha, Tarshish, Meres, Marsena, and Memucan, the seven princes of Persia and Media who had access to the king and held first place in the kingdom. [15]He asked them, "What does the law require to be done with Queen Vashti for disobeying the command of King Ahasuerus brought to her by the eunuchs?" [16]Then Memucan made answer before the king and the princes: "Queen Vashti has done wrong, and not to the king alone, but also to all the officers and to all the peoples in all the provinces of King Ahasuerus. [17]Every woman will come to know what the queen has done, and this will make them treat their husbands with contempt; they will say, 'King Ahasuerus ordered Queen Vashti to be brought before him and she did not come.' [18]The great ladies of Persia and Media, who have heard of the queen's conduct, will tell all the king's officers about this day, and there will be endless disrespect and insolence! [19]If it pleases your majesty, let a royal decree go out from you and let it be inscribed in the laws of the Persians and Medes, never to be revoked, that Vashti shall not again appear before King Ahasuerus; and let the king give her place as queen to another who is more worthy than she. [20]Thus when this royal edict is heard through the length and breadth of the kingdom, all women will give honour to their husbands, high and low alike."

> [21]Memucan's advice pleased the king and the princes, and the king did as he had proposed. [22]Letters were sent to all the royal princes, to every province in its own script and to every people in their own language, in order that each man might be master in his own house and control all his own womenfolk. (Esther 1:1–22, NEB)

There it was: "Each man [is to] be master in his own house and control all his own womenfolk." Our leader announced, "In spite of the sad context, this is God's order for families."

It was a tough evening for me. I thought I had mastered the main lines of biblical teaching about God's design of marriage and the family, but I had never contemplated that a decree crafted by a group of drunken, nervous politicians might be "God's order." I wondered whether Jesus had a word that would intersect with these dangerous men's "law." (I will return to the Lovers Lane Bible study at the opening of Chapter 9. For now, suffice it to say that I once would have accepted what the Exxon leader said, but not anymore.)

How We Did It at Home: Don's Story

Chivalry feels good—taking care of the woman! I like myself better for remembering to treat Robbie like my queen. I like walking on the gutter side of the sidewalk to protect her from the howling winds of traffic and any flying debris flung by passing cargo. I like sitting on the aisle in the church pew, lest she might be violated by some stranger crowding up against her.

The division of labor feels normal, the way it is supposed to be. My mother always made my bed and gathered my clothes that needed to be laundered. Mother had my meals ready on schedule and cleaned up afterward. And as a young husband, I rejoiced that such a clear distinction was written into the universe. Robbie seemed to like doing most of the same things my mother had done, and I did my part.

"My part" consisted of looking after everything external. I kept the car clean and serviced, ready to roll. I was eager for Robbie to learn to drive and to be licensed, but I was relieved (and our marriage likely fared better) when my thirteen-year-old sister taught her to drive the tough-shifting farm pickup. Even then, I never expected Robbie to be worried about car maintenance, oil, gas, or repairs.

I also expected to be fully responsible for supporting the new marriage and household—earning the income, banking the money, paying the bills, and keeping Robbie in a style to which she had been accustomed at home. I was built for that kind of responsibility, and it stretched me from being a boy into feeling that I was now a man in every sense of the word.

Taking Control of My Woman

Given this enormous "external responsibility" for two people, instead of just myself, I did not hesitate to make decisions for both of us. Shortly before we were married, I agreed, without consulting her, to stop off to handle the music ministry for a summer countywide revival in western Kansas, located right on our route home from our honeymoon. I said, "Yes," to the telephone invitation and, when the organizers asked whether Robbie would play the piano for the event, I also said, "Yes." Big mistake—even though she complied!

I announced the booking in my next letter, about six months ahead of the wedding. Why wasn't I surprised that she accepted my booking for her musical talent? Because this was the way the world should work. I knew her. I knew myself. And I could make decisions for both of us, anytime, anywhere.

"Head of the Family"

Our boys were born four years apart, and I initiated the timing of their births. Since I was carrying the checkbook, watching our income, and watching the calendar of our lives, it was clear that I had the necessary grasp of the best times to start and to expand our family.

Once the boys arrived, I expected Robbie to look after them and be their almost exclusive caregiver. Robbie took a temporary leave from teaching third grade and did not return to teaching until after our second son was up and running. I was glad to be the boys' father, but their meals, laundry, bedtime, and nighttime care were almost exclusively Robbie's domain. She was "Mother," and she was handling the role very well.

I read the "headship" passages in Ephesians and was warmed. They seemed to insist that wives "submit to" their husbands, and I picked up the encouragement to love Robbie "as Christ loved the church." If I did that, I believed, we were both following the submission text. I found myself formed as a male, and all of my fighting muscles twitched at the thought of how I would courageously lay down my life to protect Robbie and the babies.

I read in Paul's letters to the Corinthians, too, that women should keep silent in the church, and that they should never be permitted to teach men (1 Tim. 2:11–15). All of this matched most of what I observed in the church and gradually shaped me theologically. I thought women should do the nurturing, childcare, and early childhood teaching in the church. I was then a pastor as well as a public schoolteacher, and I observed the uncanny way that women on the elementary school faculty seemed instinctively to know what children needed. It was "mothering" extended to the larger community. But I saw that men could handle discipline objectively, acting as referees, principals, and coaches.

Suddenly, I found myself handed duties for regional, then national teaching on subjects related to family life and Christian education. By 1957, I was regularly boarding DC-6 planes. (Anybody remember them, nose up? Upon boarding, you tilted back toward the plane's tail on the ground!) I was regularly flying off to teach about the family and about the church's educational mission. I was glad to share what was working so well in my own little family and in my congregation.

Within a decade, I was sitting in a national office for my denomination, shaping the study and conceptual life of the whole church. I knew I was not prepared for such responsibility, so I arranged to begin doctoral research and study at Indiana University. My culminating research project focused on home and church curriculum experiments.[1]

I was not surprised to prove with my nicely controlled experiment in local congregations in southern Michigan that home teaching was as effective as teaching done at church. I also proved that when they were combined, they were the most effective. I had randomized gender for the experiment, but when I discovered that my research sample consisted of 62 percent girls of grades four, five, and six, and only 38 percent boys, I separated the data by sex. What I discovered has driven my remaining lifelong reflection and search for better understanding of males and females. I found that boys learned best at home and almost not at all at church, and that girls learned very well at church but not as well as boys learned at home.[2] That was in 1969.

---

[1] Donald M. Joy, *Value-Oriented Instruction in the Church and in the Home* (Bloomington: Indiana University, 1969).

[2] I reported a condensed version of the research data in "Building Children's Beliefs," *Christianity Today*, June 19, 1970.

For the next ten years, I worked under the assumption that sex differences were indeed a reality. I believed that my research indicated that the boys needed to learn how to do family headship tasks at home with their fathers, while girls could learn their maternal tasks anywhere. Besides, most of the girls' teachers at home and at church were women. When I went back ten years later to the same churches in which the research occurred, the boys still had virtually no chance of having a teacher in church who was a male. There were no male Sunday school teachers until sixth grade, if at all.

My personal experience was now fused with my professional platform, reinforced by the data from my research at Indiana University. The theory of male headship was nicely formed and easily articulated. I was wrapped in the gentlest of concerns for the protecting of women, for cushioning women from major responsibilities, so that their gracious gifts of caregiving, mothering, and loving might enhance the lives of homes and congregations and communities everywhere.

I thought this "chain of command" as taught in those days in Basic Youth Conflicts seminars far and wide was a bit harsh. Nevertheless, being the head of the home and head of the educational work of the church seemed right to me. It was so right, in fact, that I seldom thought of articulating it. I found it easy to live out and natural to make the decisions I felt were best for the family. I surprised them with decisions that involved buying new automobiles, making travel reservations for vacations, and even making career decisions that uprooted us all. It was tough work, being the head of the house, and I found myself needing to bring the family around by my persuasion and logic after my decisions were beyond changing. But they gave in to my choices. This confirmed that my way was "the way it is supposed to be."

I doubt that I could have loved Robbie and the boys any more than I did in those days before 1971. I did battle for the family in the world outside the home, and Robbie handled the household management. Even when I brought home guests unannounced, she remained poised and gracious. They were business associates who dropped in on me, and I dropped them in on her and the boys and the home. She kept an immaculate house, so I was comfortable barging in the front door with guests in tow.

Robbie and I were gracious to each other, obviously lovers in every way. We reared our family on the second pew front, on the left—partly because I often had platform responsibility with music and worship, but also because that is where I grew up loving to sit with Grandpa and Grandma Joy. I was made for this. I was head of my house. We have never talked about it much, but now I'm asking Robbie to tell you how it actually felt to live in this "father-dominated" family.

How it Felt at Home: Robbie's Story

In our family with its two daughters, it was easy to see my dad as "lord and king" of our castle. He never demanded special treatment, but he was so different from the three of us women that his six-foot-two hulk appearing in midafternoon was enough to send us into orbit. He was the "savior of the home" in a literal as well as an ideal sense. He managed to stay up with us until bedtime and read stories to us, even though he had to be up at 4:30 A.M.—off to deliver mail for the Dallas, Texas, post office carrier system every weekday. We even shared a whole family bedroom until Johnetta and I were in our teens.

My mother never was on a payroll. She ruled our home in a benevolent way, but it was Daddy that Mother slaved to feed and groom and to send off into the world outside, there to battle the world, the flesh, and the devil. Dad even did the grocery shopping. He was unwilling to drive a car (we think because of some frightening early experience while he was away in Europe during World War I), but Dad offered to buy a car if "Ree" would learn to drive it. She did. He took responsibility for negotiating its maintenance, but Mother always had to drive it to the station or the garage.

"My Lord, Don"

I could not have been more pleased at moving from the care of Dad into the total care of my husband. I was glad to see that Don expected to take care of earning the money, paying the bills, and deciding what we could afford at any given moment. What a relief it was to be free to do what I loved to do: to keep house, think about interior decorating, add nice touches around the house, keeping the home fresh and clean, cherishing the almost daily laundry, and returning everything to its "place." I didn't need to worry, hardly even to think. It never occurred to me to "decide" about whether I would go to church, to a convention that Don was scheduled to attend, or to help his parents with harvest-time farming. It was enough that Don had considered all of the issues of time, priority, and other moral questions for us. If he said it, I did it. It never occurred to me to raise a question about whether, like God's creation, things were "good."

In the early years of our marriage, when the boys were small, I could count on it: When Don came home, he took over at home. He could make my day simply by walking through the door. I could tell him how exasperated I was, and he would walk right into the situation and peace would reign. He could be playful or firm and direct with the boys, and they always responded to him in a magical way. Rarely was I sorry to have waited for him to solve a domestic crisis only to find that he came out with a different judgment from what I had formed. In those instances, I sometimes felt betrayed because I felt he had sided with one of the boys instead of me. But then I got over those feelings. Don was omniscient, not me. Eventually, I would blame myself for not having "seen it" his way earlier, and I would go on quite content with our roles.

Deliverance and Protection

My husband was my defender and protector. If I had taken some criticism during the parsonage years, both in Kansas and in Texas, he would soothe me and slay the dragon that bit me. And in those early years, when the same telephone that came to the house served the church office as well, I picked up some church calls when he was out. I was proud of him when he informed the secretary of the official board in the church that she was never again to take out her anger on me. And she didn't.

When the decision came to leave teaching school in Minneola, Kansas, for Don to study at Asbury Theological Seminary in Kentucky, I was ready. Don was called to ministry, and of course, we must go. I recall that he, as the total protector, went through all of the channels by which he could be appointed as pastor of the Lexington Free Methodist Church. There were serious faith leaps for us, given the lack of a parsonage there, and the income would be pretty thin. When we arrived, Don learned that, instead of earning a seminary degree in three years, we were looking at a slow and scenic trip of five instead. And the projected income for full-time ministry would mean that we would have neither vacation time nor the necessary gas money to visit our family in Texas and Kansas. At that, I felt my first chunk of mild terror. My powerful knight in shining armor had made decisions that brought us far from home. We were now living on a thin shoestring, and we were facing a challenge of survival. Because we had a nine-month-old son, Don pursued this pastoral option so that I would not have to work outside the home. There seemed to be "no other way."

My Liberator

I dropped out of college at seventeen, after my second year, to earn enough money to float our wedding. That was the bride's responsibility. It never occurred to me to challenge the prevalent cultural idea that a grand wedding was paid for by the bride or her parents. Don had been unable to understand why the cost of a wedding would take me out of college, but he knew that my tuition would be his responsibility when we were married the next year. My parents were relieved to know that, too. It never occurred to Don, to me, or to my parents to discuss the possibility that my parents would continue to support my education after I was married. Don was my provider. His parents could back him—and us, if there was an emergency. But I was emancipated entirely from my father's support and care.

It was Don who talked to me about having a dream of what I would like to do as an adult career after the children were up and in school. Our experience in that brief career of teaching on emergency-provisional certificates at Minneola, Kansas, allowed me to see how well I was matched to teaching. Don kept alive my dream of graduating and being certified to teach. He often spoke of my college degree as our "insurance policy," in the event I should lose Don. His ever-watchful concern could not contemplate my being left without a means of earning a living, should some catastrophe take him. His utilitarian reasoning and my vocational dream matched, so I graduated in 1952—three years after we should have graduated together, had I not dropped out to work for the wedding expenses.

Across the years, Don continued to urge me on. In Texas, as I was going berserk from cabin fever in a parsonage with one young son and another on the way, Don urged me to begin a master's degree program at East Texas State University. My degrees leapfrogged Don's, and each time he urged me on. So when Don began his doctoral study at Indiana University, Don encouraged me to put my energy where my occasional dream took me and complete a reading specialist certificate. That rigorous program was another thirty hours of graduate study and we managed to enroll in a couple of classes together. Even there, Don was my support and my strength. He came to our campus apartment one summer day to find me almost wild as I tried in vain to type a paper for a course we shared on personality theory. Even though he was buried in papers and reading, he transformed my rough notes into a paper so good that the professor asked for a copy to put in the library reserve as a model for future classes. That was ironic. And I was deeply embarrassed because Don had written his own paper for the same class. It just wasn't right that I outperformed my husband, in his own field, and that I used him as my personal secretary and typist.

The Best of All Possible Worlds?

When the man protects the home castle and its weak and helpless woman and children, how could anything be better or safer in all the world? Everywhere in 1960s America the logic was reinforced. The strong must protect the weak. Women are relatively weaker than men, and therefore must be prevented even from trying to protect themselves. Men are larger and heavier, and therefore must use their size and strength to shield, to cover, and to care for the smaller and lighter females and their offspring.

A benevolent monarchy is the most efficient and generous arrangement in any human society. The recipients have little responsibility but large reward, depending on the fortunes of the king and on his wisdom in judgments affecting their wealth and comfort. So also the vertical household provides maximum benefits with minimum responsibilities for everybody except good old Dad, who brings home not only the bacon, but also the other goods and money that are essential for the family to live lives of extravagant consumption and pleasure.

Besides, "good old Dad" loves the role of omnipotent, omniscient breadwinner and pleasure giver. He feels ten feet tall if he can surprise the family with some generous gift, especially if it signals a new level of accomplishment and success status, which is an accomplishment for the entire family. His annual bonus can buy an extravagant round of Christmas gifts or a special ski holiday for the family. His "devotion to the cause"— being gone days and nights, most evenings and weekends—means he is doing his duty for his family. He takes a second job or starts up an entrepreneurial sideline, then burns midnight oil to get it going, because he is improving the quality of life for the woman and children he loves.

Good old Mom tends the home fires, earns her favors by the sweat of her brow as she manages children, runs the car pool, does the laundry, and redecorates the house. She negotiates with the garbage collection crew over problems in service, collects the bills for Dad to pay, buys the groceries, makes beds, and keeps the house immaculate. She gets the children's school, meal, and transportation schedules worked out and executes them. She keeps the community safe for children and for herself, helps sell Girl Scout cookies, and goes door-to-door on the drive to build an extension on the public library. She attends PTA, sees that the children are in Sunday school or catechism classes, and makes sure that the whole family shows up scrubbed and shining in the Sunday morning worship pew. She does all of this for her husband. It is her gift to him. She adores him, justifies his frequent trips away, defends him, and considers herself lucky to have his affection, his attention, and his generous backing and financial support.

Dad is unaware of any other possible world of marriage and family, and Mom is oblivious, too. Theirs is assumed to have been the eternal pattern for marriage from Adam and Eve to Old Testament heroes to modern teachers on family structure in the church. Paul speaks of "headship" in the family, so Christians must understand all of this and reaffirm it. The pattern is seen everywhere in nature—the animals, the birds, and the bees. And in every primitive society, the pattern seems to reappear: Men are the gatherers, while women bear children and tend the fires at the home base. Of course, polygamy keeps popping up in ancient and modern times; but that is not necessarily a sign of any flaw in "God's order for families." Or is it?

Why Does the Vertical Marriage Work So Well?

A sensitive, vertical couple form an almost indestructible unit. Each one's expectations of the other match. Conflict is at a minimum. They can play their traditional roles without asking deep and profound questions about the value of persons, the dignity of personhood, or about the losses they are all sustaining by their verticalizing of the marriage.

But the vertical marriage works well primarily because it matches the fallen configuration of man's and woman's personality structure and instinctual aspirations. Here are those synchronized "deformities" of men and women:

Woman: Her "desire" (that is, her "worship") shall be focused on her husband.

Man: He "shall rule over" the woman.

Why does this hierarchical, curse-based marriage work so well? It is because it is the "natural" model of fallen humanity. It matches our symbiotic deformities and we feel "normal" together. It works especially well when the two partners have been made gentle by faith or sheer civility. The kind, benevolent male who is joined with the compliant and affectionate female easily forms a glorious "castle" for his home. His wife is his queen and Christ is his Lord. The husband stands between the woman and God as her intercessor and her representation of God's supreme role as husband, groom, and father. How could anything so beautiful and so efficient be flawed?

Yearning for the More Excellent Way

Robbie and I stood with the pastoral couple on Father's Day, 1985, following morning worship at First United Methodist Church in Tulsa, Oklahoma. I had preached in three identical worship services, and only after the final one was the luxury of greeting worshipers possible. As worshipers were making their exit past this clergy and spouse lineup, I noticed one middle-aged couple repeatedly going to the back of the line. I speculated that either they wanted more time for greeting the clergy, or that they did not want to embarrass themselves by speaking while others waited and watched. When they greeted us, the woman in tears seemed unable to speak. Her husband said:

"We joined this church a year ago because we had come to the end of our rope at a great Bible church here in Tulsa. We raised our family there, but we never quite found a way to make their teachings match our marriage and life as a family. It always insisted that the husband is the lone ranger and that he rules and controls everyone else.

"Somehow we just knew that the teaching was wrong, but they were proudly teaching it 'from the Bible.' It was a church that surely held the Bible very high. Still, we knew this teaching was wrong. Our own experience across the years told us the teaching was wrong.

"So we left that church and joined here, but we did so with a sense of sadness—of loss. We felt that we had left the Bible behind. But this morning you gave it back to us."

By then they were both full of tears, as Robbie and I were. We grieved that "fallen" men and women are told to remain as they are by equally deformed Bible teachers, preachers, and authors who look through distorted lenses until the Scriptures seem to match their deformed pattern for marriage and families. When they have finished their work, they boldly announce it as "God's plan for families."

I had preached that morning a sermon I had called "Creation, Adam, and Woman." It is now easily available in *Bonding: Relationships in the Image of God.* I could not have preached that sermon before 1980, so I am well-qualified to line up for my share of repentance along with any of you who may be inclined to embrace the hierarchical marriage and family as your model because it is "natural."

Today, Robbie and I are quietly sure that such models are not God's original design or God's present intention. We continue to unfold the cultural wrappings that conceal the mystery of "two become one" who jointly "have dominion." On a day-do-day basis, we embrace the rich life that this Creation-Jesus-Paul way of living and working provides. The breakthrough has come only by confronting the big picture of Scripture, with heavy doses of repentance and exciting but painful learning.

In this chapter we wanted to show you how well adapted we were for the traditional vertical marriage. We are very much products of having been through the entire pilgrimage of our marriage, and this is an important chapter in it.

Questions People Ask

Q. *I find your ideas about co-regency and your typing your wife's paper very upsetting. My wife is satisfied with our arrangement, and we both try to follow the "chain of command" the best we can. She does the child care and the household work like typing, and I earn the living and pay the bills. Why are you trying to confuse the issues when so many people agree with us?*

A. We have not written this book or told our story to upset anyone—least of all folks who are enjoying their hierarchical marriages as we did for several decades. But some desperate folks long for a fully empowering marriage and family life, and a few are so discouraged that they are quietly wondering how to get out of marriage all together. We are quite sure we can walk with them into a rich and fully biblically grounded life together.

But for you, we want you to close this book and lay it aside. Get on with your best understanding of your obedience to Jesus and your walk with God. If you ever have second thoughts about your present "chain of command" marriage, you may want to pick the book up again. We believe you will be rewarded when you trade in your present model of marriage for what we are calling here the co-regent model.

5

Tragic Losses:
"...And He Shall Rule Over Her"

Polly escaped to Dallas when Dan began pursuing a mistress again. His impressive career required that he keep an apartment near the state capitol, but Dan and Polly's home was fifty miles away. I had met Polly in an Ichthus seminar I taught one spring in Wilmore, and later worked with Dan to search for a path to fidelity. Sometime later, I realized I had a long layover in Dallas as I was en route to teach in Los Angeles.

"I'm flying to Los Angeles to do some concentrated teaching in a doctoral program," I told Polly's mother, whose phone number Polly had left with us. "If Polly can get away, I have a three-hour layover." I gave the Delta flight number for my Dallas arrival.

When I stepped through the arrival gate, there was Polly. We walked to my departure area and sat there for the entire layover. I was not prepared for Polly's current questions:

"Sometimes I think I was wrong to insist that Dan be exclusively faithful to me. I wonder if my goals were unrealistic. When I read about King David in the Old Testament, 'a man after [God's] own heart' (1 Sam. 13:14), I notice that he had several wives. He even had children by many of them. And I think, *That's what Dan wanted, and I wouldn't let him have it. I forced him to choose between Betty and me.*"

Her question stung like an arrow: "Did I do wrong when I insisted that Dan had to be faithful to me or I would have to leave?"

I took out a notepad and drew a three-level diagram that compares God's design in Creation, human losses in the Genesis 3 tragic Fall, and Jesus' redemption, which opens the way to higher fidelity and holiness than Creation knew.

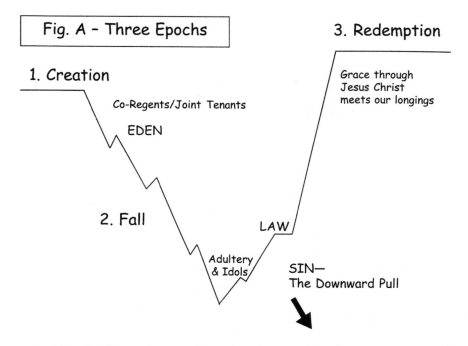

I told Polly, "Your dream of marriage is rooted in the Creation. It is the universal longing of honest men and women—exclusive, lifelong, 'two-become-one' living." Then pointing to "Redemption" on my chart, I said, "Jesus has ushered in a grand recovery that sets an even higher potential to that 'two-become-one' vision that honest and healthy folks have. All sorts of things have been done to eliminate polygamy, murder of unloved spouses, and prostitution to help more and more people claim the dream with the support of social and political structures for their marriages and security for their families."

Then pointing to the chasm created by the "Fall" in Eden, I went on: "But King David appeared in history at a time when things were 'in the pits.' God is always able to work through imperfect people. So King David was 'God's man' of the hour for turning the people's hearts back toward faithfulness to their national identity and their mission. But David's life was complicated and his family was devastated by his adultery, his murder to get a woman, and his polygamy. Those tragic features of his fallen culture might never have crossed his mind, since he was trapped in a culture that believed that hierarchical, 'chain-of-command' marriages should silence the women.

"Our problem," I suggested to Polly, "is this. We too live in a world that in many ways is still warped by the sin that ended Eden. We look around us and see the tragic patterns of sexual behavior and the destruction of families, and it is easy for us to say, 'That's normal, so I guess my life is not so bad.' And these seductions of our vision can take our eyes off the call to live holy lives in the midst of an unholy world."

I reminded Polly that she was the only one who could say whether her marriage to Dan could survive. I told her that God's vision was for a "one-flesh," "naked and unashamed," "two-become-one" marriage for a lifetime. But in no case, I assured her, was she obligated to return "to the pits" of Old Testament polygamy with its devastating sexual and social consequences. Nor should she imagine that overlooking Dan's persistent adulteries would be "more Christian."

From Intimacy to Adversaries

From the beautiful images of Creation's marital bond—"two become one," one flesh, naked and unashamed—the scene deteriorated to self-protecting, self-indulgent sin. And from the intimacy of the first Man and Woman, walking with God in the Garden in the cool of the day, the relationship with God was fractured by disobedience, rebellion, and their consequences: shame and guilt. The tragedy of disobedience to God's best word to man and woman unfolds this way in Genesis 3:

> [1]Now the serpent was more cunning than any beast of the field which the LORD God had made. [2]And he said to the woman, "Has God indeed said, 'You shall not eat of every tree of the garden'?" And the woman said to the serpent, "We may eat the fruit of the trees of the garden; [3]but of the fruit of the tree which is in the midst of the garden, God has said, 'You shall not eat it, nor shall you touch it, lest you die.'" [4]Then the serpent said to the woman. "You will not surely die. [5]For God knows that in the day you eat of it your eyes will be opened, and you will be like God, knowing good and evil." [6]So when the woman saw that the tree *was* good for food, that *was* pleasant to the eyes, and a tree desirable to make *one* wise, she took of its fruit and ate. She also gave to her husband with her,

and he ate. [7]Then the eyes of both of them were opened, and they knew that they *were* naked; and they sewed fig leaves together and made themselves coverings. [8]And they heard the sound of the LORD God walking in the garden in the cool of the day, and Adam and his wife hid themselves from the presence of the LORD God among the trees of the garden.

[9]Then the LORD God called to Adam and said to him, "Where *are* you?" [10]So he said, "I heard Your voice in the garden, and I was afraid because I was naked; and I hid myself." [11]And He said, "Who told you that you *were* naked? Have you eaten from the tree of which I commanded you that you should not eat?" [12]Then the man said, "The woman whom You gave *to be* with me, she gave me of the tree, and I ate." [13]And the LORD God said to the woman, "What *is* this you have done?" The woman said, "The serpent deceived me, and I ate." [14]So the LORD God said to the serpent:

> "Because you have done this,
> You are cursed more than all cattle,
> And more than every beast of the field;
> On your belly you shall go,
> And you shall eat dust
> All the days of your life.
> [15]And I will put enmity
> Between you and the woman,
> And between your seed and her Seed;
> He shall bruise your head,
> And you shall bruise his heel."

[16]To the woman He said:
> "I will greatly multiply your sorrow and your conception;
> In pain you shall bring forth children;
> Your desire *shall be* for your husband,
> And he shall rule over you."

[17]Then to Adam He said, "Because you have heeded the voice of your wife, and have eaten from the tree of which I commanded you, saying, 'You shall not eat of it':

"Cursed *is* the ground for your sake;
In toil you shall eat *of* it
All the days of your life.
[18]Both thorns and thistles it shall bring forth for you,
And you shall eat the herb of the field.
[19]In the sweat of your face you shall eat bread
Till you return to the ground,
For out of it you were taken;
For dust you *are*,
And to dust you shall return."

[20]And Adam called his wife's name Eve, because she was the mother of all living. [21]Also for Adam and his wife the LORD God made tunics of skin, and clothed them.

[22]Then the LORD God said, "Behold, the man has become like one of Us, to know good and evil. And now, lest he put out his hand and take also of the tree of life, and eat, and live forever"—[23]therefore the LORD God sent him out of the garden of Eden to till the ground from which he was taken. [24]So He drove out the man; and He placed cherubim at the east of the garden of Eden and a flaming sword which turned every way, to guard the way to the tree of life.

Notice the unfolding of God's relationship with humanity, and of the relationship between man and woman:

1. The Lord God opens the door for humanity to creatively manage the whole creation with the exception of "the tree of the knowledge of good and evil" (that is, "knowing" by experimenting, instead of by trusting God's wisdom). [1] The warning is clear: "In the day that you eat of it you shall surely die" (Gen. 2:17).

---

[1]William M. Logan, *In the Beginning, God* (Richmond, Va.: John Knox Press, 1957), notes that "Interpretation of [the meaning of 'The tree of the knowledge of good and evil'] requires careful attention to the Hebrew concepts that are employed. 'Knowledge' must be understood in the biblical rather than 'academic' or 'theoretical" sense of knowledge" (p. 34). "To know," in the case of marriage, meant to explore and develop intimate acquaintance by experimentation.

2. The serpent challenges the man and the woman at the one point of exception: "Has God said, 'You shall not eat of every tree of the garden'?" (Gen. 3:1).

3. The Woman (not called Eve yet, but *Ishshah* or Woman) correctly recites the taboo (Gen. 3:2–3).

4. The serpent asserts that God has lied: "You will not surely die. For God knows that in the day you eat of it your eyes will be opened, and you will be like God, knowing good and evil"—by experience instead of by command or intuition (Gen. 3:4–5).

5. The woman, softened by the serpent's assertion, observes the visual attractiveness of the fruit of the forbidden tree: It "was good for food…it was pleasant to the eyes, and a tree desirable to make one wise." So she "took of its fruit and ate" (Gen. 3:6).

6. "She also gave to her husband with her, and he ate" (Gen. 3:6). Contrary to the common idea that her husband was somewhere else and didn't know what he was eating, the text suggests that he was standing right there with her when she took the fruit.

7. "Then the eyes of both of them were opened, and they knew that they *were* naked" (Gen. 3:7). This denotes the awakening of human shame, not guilt. The couple's sudden shock was one of being "exposed," not one of remorse for having gone against God's plan for them. Guilt will come some generations later. Shame evokes physical, tangible symptoms of inferiority, incompetence, and worthlessness—hence their hiding. Guilt triggers confession, an eagerness to "make things right," and it induces a person to own personal responsibility for the disobedience. There is no possibility of repentance when shame is the response to failure or disobedience. Only guilt leads to honest sorrow for failure and opens the door to walking with God in transforming holiness and righteousness.[2]

8. The shame intensifies as *Ish* and *Ishshah* (Man and Woman) hear "the sound of the LORD God walking in the garden in the cool of the day,

---

[2] For a further discussion of the narcissism and egocentrism of shame that renders it incapable of repentance until it can be transformed into guilt, see "Naked and Unashamed: The Universal Longing," in my book *Re-bonding: Preventing and Restoring Broken Relationships* (Nappanee, Ind.: Evangel Publishing House, 2000), pp. 42–43.

and Adam and his wife hid themselves from the presence of the LORD God among the trees of the garden" (Gen. 3:8).

9. The LORD God calls out, "Adam! Where *are* you?" (Gen. 3:9).[3] An alternate translation to underscore the solidarity of the original Adam might be to have the LORD God crying out, "Adam! Where are both of you?" Such a question, in any event, denotes a fracture in the primary relationship with God. How very different our picture of God would be if He had cried out first, "What is this that you have done?" God's first cry to humans is always one of grief over losing us. We were created for intimacy with God. God's search for us is the story of all of human history since that first disobedience. Any programs of evangelism or outreach that move on any other first principle are not based on God's priority of relationships. Strategies that imply that God "uses" people, even in the name of the highest religious goals, are expressions of our own deep mark of selfishness rising out of sin.

10. In response to God's cry, "Adam! Where are you?" the man answers: "I heard Your voice in the garden, and I was afraid because I was naked; and I hid myself" (Gen. 3:10). Here "Adam" is claimed by the man as his exclusive name. God's call to "Adam" may have been to the full Adam of Creation—male and female, the species name. But the male answers, and his answer is completely self-protecting. Shame triggers "blame." So the woman is blamed, and the man makes no effort to own disobedience for himself. Speaking only for himself, he names fear and shame as his condition.

11. God offers the man a way to convert his shame to honest guilt. If he had accepted God's invitation, then he would have made a full confession of disobedience: 'Who told you that you *were* naked?' God asked. 'Have you eaten from the tree of which I commanded you that you should not eat?' (Gen. 3 :11). Perhaps the entire history of self-protecting blaming and denial could have been avoided if only the first Man leaped across the chasm of fear and shame. Imagine how different life could have been for all of us if he had simply said, "Yes. I violated Your command. Was it You who spoke to me from deep inside my head? Was it Your Spirit, who You breathed into me at

---

[3]Consult the Hebrew text or an interlinear version where you can see the "Adam" language.

Creation, who exposed my failure and showed me how vulnerable and naked I was?"

12. But the man commits the original act of blaming: "The woman whom You gave *to be* with me, she gave me of the tree, and I ate" (Gen. 3:12). The truth comes out: Man, who seems to have watched *Ishshah's* visual and logical seduction, made no gesture toward restraining her. Instead, he now attempts to make his disobedience her full responsibility. He pushes it even farther. He blames God, because it was God's design to draw woman from the Adam and complete the mystery of "two become one." That mystery will now be under severe strain. Blaming is the oldest weapon a spouse can use to attack God's gift of intimate Trinitarian community.

13 The Lord God then turns to *Ishshah*, Woman: "What *is* this you have done?" (Gen. 3:13). God offers separate opportunities for guilt-based confession and repentance to Man and to Woman. The dialogue reminds us of our parenting, when we try to unravel what went wrong in the play yard.

14. "The woman said, 'The serpent deceived me, and I ate'" (Gen. 3:13). So the moving finger now points blame at the serpent, whose seductive words awakened the visual curiosity and the chain of multiple disobedience that took down both Woman and Man. Woman's sin was to accept the serpent deception. Man's sin, it would seem from the text, was a willful, sentient, eyes-wide-open rebellion.

15. Skip ahead to the painful conclusion: "And Adam called his wife's name Eve, because she was the mother of all living. Also for Adam and his wife the LORD God made tunics of skin, and clothed them" (Gen. 3:20–21). At first Man (*Ish*) had spoken of Woman (*Ishshah*) as "bone of my bones, flesh of my flesh," celebrating the mystery of "two become one"! But here all of that has collapsed. Woman has instrumental value, not intimacy and shared dominion. We will come back to this later.

Curses and Consequences

What follows, then, in swift succession are three vivid word pictures that make clear where curses and consequences fall on the players. They apply to the three principals in the tragedy: the serpent, Woman, and Man. The sequence matches their appearance in the drama and their active participation in what we have come to call the original sin. Note that, just as Woman and Man respond to the seduction in differing ways, their motivations are also different. Hence, we will see differences in their consequences. Once "two become one" in full solidarity, they are now separate in their culpability and in the consequences for their disobedience.

The serpent is cursed, and the soil or ground is cursed. Revisit Genesis 3:14–15 and 17–18 and celebrate the fact that Woman and Man are not cursed. The physical structure of the serpent is changed by the curse, suggesting that any images we have of the agent from hell are inadequate.[4] An adversary relationship has been struck between the serpent and humankind. Check the instinctual response in the back of your neck and in your pulse rate the next time you overtake a snake—and pray that one never overtakes you! Our responses to snakes differ dramatically from those on encountering virtually any other species. Thus, the Genesis curse on the serpent makes sense to us at an intuitive level, even though the story itself may leave us baffled as we search for meaning through the strange images.

In a remarkable prophecy by Isaiah, the alienation that comes down in Genesis 3 is reversed and the sixth-day species are reconciled:

> [6]The wolf shall live with the lamb,
> > the leopard shall lie down with the kid,
> The calf and the lion and the fatling together,
> > and a little child shall lead them.
> [7]The cow and the bear shall graze,
> > their young shall lie down together;
> > and the lion shall eat straw like the ox.
> [8]The nursing child shall play over the hole of the asp,
> > and the weaned child shall put its hand on the adder's den,
> [9]They will not hurt or destroy
> > on all my holy mountain;

---

[4] I grew up in Meade County, Kansas, where rattlesnakes were abundant. Once when Dad had killed one, he called me close to see the dimpled rows along the underside. "There is where the feet once were, Donny," he said. It was credible. But imagine my shock to read that all snakes carry a "pelvic girdle" about two-thirds of the way down their spines. Showing a group of us a specimen in a museum, one curator said calmly, "It is clear that snakes once had legs." My point here is only to suggest that there is a lost sense of what or how this serpent worked in this primal story.

> For the earth will be full of the knowledge of the LORD
> As the waters cover the sea. (Isa. 11:6–9, NRSV)

John Wesley, in his published sermon "The Brute Creation," cites the solidarity of the species because of human sin. He observes that all species have been marked by fear and alienation, and that the ultimate reconciliation of all creatures awaits God's special deliverance. He cites this passage from Isaiah 11.

The soil is cursed. At Creation, God charged Man and Woman together to have dominion and creative management of the entire earth and its creatures. But that was a friendly creation. Now alienation has struck Man and Woman and their relationship. Trust is contaminated, being replaced by fear between humans and animals. In this alienating spiral, Man grasps the challenges of transforming the earth and its products into food, shelter, and tools as his domain. Now everything has a tendency toward chaos instead of toward order, toward death instead of toward life. These tendencies appear to spring out of the second curse: "Cursed is the ground for your sake" (likely, "because of you") (Gen. 3:17).

Painful consequences come to Woman. Look at the text again. The woman is not cursed, but the Lord God warns her of tragic consequences: (1) She will have greatly increased pain in childbirth—here called "sorrow" or "travail," twice repeated in Genesis 3:16. (2) She will have greatly multiplied conception. (3) Her "desire" shall be for her husband. And (4) her husband will rule over her. The consequences that Woman faces all deal with her most cherished relationships. Conception and childbearing are still a major fulfillment to a woman, and a source of alienation and power struggles with her husband, with whom she longs to "become one."

Managing reproductive frequency and multiplied complications in delivering human children seem straightforward, and they may open up questions to pursue for a long time. But the final two consequences strike us in chilling ways:

Woman's "desire" here is a baffling term. Most men would feel that a woman's increased "desire" for her husband would be a blessing, not a painful consequence of her disobedience. But if you contemplate the fact that the same Hebrew word is used to denote "desire" as worship, the woman's pain comes into focus. "You alone are my heart's desire, and I long to worship you," rings in our ears as a Scripture song celebrating the desire to fix our hearts on God. Woman was created, as was Man, for the worship of God and God alone. But following the disobedience, Woman now shifts to the adoration and worship of her Man. This tendency will deteriorate into a new name for "husband." He becomes "Baal," my idol, my God-substitute. Even today, Israeli women use *Baal* as the common word for "husband." Woman tends to depend too much on Man for her value and her purpose in life. She also expects perfection from him, absolute deliverance. Thus she turns against her husband when her Baal fails. Remember the classic words of Rachel by which she accuses Jacob of denying her the longing of her heart to have his child: "Give me children, or else I die!" This triggers an objection from Jacob, "Am I in the place of God?" (Gen. 30: 11).[5]

"He shall rule over you" grieves over the line now drawn between Woman and Man. Once co-regents, celebrating the unity of "two become one" in the image of the Holy Trinity, they will experience conflict between them. Man will overpower Woman and will expect to control her. The pattern is so common in all generations and in every culture that anyone could observe that it is "the natural way." But, tragically, that is because it is contaminated. It is "natural"—not Creation's design or God's will or the Jesus way. From kitchen to pulpit and everywhere in between, the perceptions of Woman and of Man gravitate toward "traditional" roles. Scriptures are read selectively and with a bias that corrupts the clear teaching of passages on submission. Remember, the Holy Spirit inspired humans to write Scripture in a special revelation, and the Greek word for "submit" does not even appear in the oldest and best manuscripts of Ephesians 5:22, although it is translated, "Wives, submit to your own husbands." Instead the verb for "submit" appears only in 5:1: "Submit to one another out of reverence for Christ." Then follow two ways submission works: "Wives, to your husbands. . . . Husbands lay down your lives for your wives. . . . "

Woman gets a new name. Once she was *Ishshah*, the mirror "other half" of the split Adam *Ish*. Check the text above once more. Now *Ishshah* is renamed by *Ish*, who takes the name of "Adam" for himself. Her new name provides no clue that there is a significant relationship between woman and man. She becomes "Eve."

---

[5]For careful reflection on "desire" and Woman's worship of man as a result of disobedience, see Walter C. Kaiser, "Your Desire Will Be for Your Husband," Chapter 6 in *Hard Sayings of the Old Testament* (Colorado Springs: Inter-Varsity Press, 1988), pp. 33 ff.

You Can Have a Marriage Where Everybody Loses!

Many marriages begin in a naive "first stage" of innocent mutuality, co-regency, and joint tenancy. The marriage partners begin by seeing themselves as sovereigns who gladly merge their kingdoms, enlarge their boundaries to include the other. But most marriages too soon enter the adversarial "second stage." The partners blame each other for misunderstandings, push for "rights" at the expense of the other, "get even," and plot to hurt each other. Many, many marriages reach a final "ruptured stage" of abuse, exploitation, and irreconcilable abandonment.

With so many marriages deteriorating quickly into the second or even into the third stage, no wonder children grow up doubting that the mystery of "two become one" ever was present for their parents. They often imagine that their parents never experienced the perfect love they are discovering.

Widespread in modern Western culture, "live-together" couples sometimes observe that when their friends marry, they begin to treat each other shabbily, just as members of the older generation do. One couple confided to us that this pattern was proof that it was better not to marry. "We couldn't imagine ever treating each other the way these friends do after they get married," they said. Their critique prompts us to examine our relationships to see whether we have followed our vision and gone deep into God's design for marriages.

Let us admit that the "adversary" marriage comes at a very high price. Here is a beginning cost sheet:

1. Lord Acton is credited with observing, "Power corrupts, and absolute power corrupts absolutely."[6] In this tragic shift for both Man and Woman, it is not surprising that Man is most often the visible offender. The husband may take care and make decisions for both of them, perhaps even in a sincere commitment to be all that his wife needs. Or he may become domineering and coercive, regarding his wife as slave and sex object, a prisoner held hostage in his home to bear and rear his children. But since a power crisis is present, Woman often discovers indirect ways to seize power. So the wife may manipulate her husband through calculated weakness, exaggerated dependency, or whining. All of these tactics frustrate his work and world. She may even regard her husband as her trophy, an endless supplier of cash and credit. In fact, it is common to see these "matching deformities" played like a dance of descending affection. Their deep

---

[6]This statement has been attributed to Lord Acton, in *Letter to Bishop Mandel Creighton*, 1887.

longings have been put on hold. Getting through a day, a week, a year, or "until the kids are up and out of the house" becomes the couple's short-term goal.

2. A woman or man who is regarded as mere "property"—a good catch, a handsome or beautiful partner—tends to remain a moral and intellectual dwarf. The "kept woman" may be protected and funded by her man, but the fact that she is locked away from the outer world guarantees that she will feel that she is forever a child. Either men or women who are unwilling or unable to take responsibility for their own lives tend to be unable to make "final moral choices" at a principled level.[7]

What I describe here as a common experience for women occurs also for any members of a social or ethnic group who for any reason are not allowed to take major responsibility for themselves. Children, for example, who are prevented from making any final moral choices until they leave home for college or military service or employment tend not to be ready to make mature moral decisions. The college freshmen year, therefore, is littered with the ruins that result when young men and women suddenly must learn moral responsibility on a grand scale where the stakes are very high. Shared mutual responsibility is critical if a family is to become an environment in which everyone learns wisdom by experience under careful support and supervision.

So the bad news is clear: There is a central tendency in all of us to allow our innocent dreams of intimacy and "two-become-one" marriage to give way to antagonism and emotional battle scars. Unless we get a clear perception of the difference between "the way things are" and "the way things were meant to be," we can be sure that all of us will know a lot of pain and forfeit the best and holiest gifts of life.

In this chapter, we have wanted you to weep with us at the enormous losses we all experience with the first Man and Woman. However, we can recapture the vision that drives our deepest hungers. We can be transformed to the extent that each of us is able to confess either that "I am man, but tragically a 'son of Adam' with destructive tendencies toward dominance and control," or that "I am woman, but painfully and truly a 'daughter of

---

[7]Several psychologists have confirmed Jean Piaget's groundbreaking research in the 1930s to observe ways in which people "make meaning" of their life experiences and potentially turn them into wisdom. Among them are Lawrence Kohlberg, Carol Gilligan, and Robert Kegan.

Eve' with self-destructive tendencies to depend too much on a man for identity and to substitute my man for the living God."

So we acknowledge that we were made with the vision of Creation in our heads. Let us affirm too that Jesus is going to recapture that dream through the transforming and reconciling grace He provides, but let us do the harder thing: Let us now decide to tell the truth in our marriages and families and relationships, to own full responsibility for our central tendencies to sin against each other. Let us confess our tendency to become adversaries, to blame and to shame each other, to savor stereotypical jokes about the other, and to avoid at all costs owning sin's fault and offense as our very own.

Questions People Ask

Q. *For eighteen years, now with several children, I have always known that God loved my husband and heard him when he prayed. But I have never had any assurance that God cared about me. My husband has made literally all of the decisions, right down to the number and timing of the children I would bear. Is it possible that "my desire for my husband" may have set him up to "rule over me" and that is part of the reason that I sometimes don't even feel like a person?*

A. You surely may have put your finger on the reason. Self-esteem is not entirely the result of what somebody else does to us, but all of us—men as well as women—suffer from feelings of inadequacy, inferiority, and absence of self-respect. Find some trusted person with whom to discuss these issues, a person who knows you and your family situation. It will be important for your husband's sake as well as yours that you come "on board" with your own direct sense of being created Woman in the image of God.

Q. *I am twenty-eight years old, and frankly, I am a little afraid to date women. It seems there simply aren't any of the old kind left—like my mother, for example. She lives for Daddy and really makes life good for him and for me. I'm still at home. Are you saying in this chapter that there is something wrong with having a woman simply there "to take care of you" and to devote her whole life to just being your wife?*

A. Many women have presented just such a "gift" to their husbands. They, and many women today, some of them very mature, sense that their vocation and calling is to be wife and mother. But a husband and a wife should present themselves to each other as gifts. If you are either waiting or actually searching for such a good, "functional" wife, you are very close to reducing all women to service objects—to mere property. And there is a problem facing a woman whose "vocation" is wife and mother, and that alone. Such women will complete their "mother" role and still have decades of life beyond childbearing and child launching. One of the greatest challenges to Christian families fifty years ago was the depression that occurred at midlife for women. These were women whose purpose in life had seemed to disappear because they were no longer bringing babies into the world and mothering them.

Go ahead. Be a man of righteousness and affection. Be ready to respond to a good woman whose heart is fixed on God. Then share your dreams, hopes, and vision, and find a way to develop your marriage relationship as co-regents, both submitting to God and to each other, and be prepared for a dynamic marriage that changes with the challenges.

Q. *There has been a sort of scandal in our part of the country. There was a pastor who led about half of a fine congregation in establishing a new independent church. Most of the people who went with him are widows, fractured families, and some convicted drug addicts. He now dominates their lives. Are some people more susceptible to the Genesis 3 distortions than others?*

A. It is possible that you are on to something. You can find this sort of pattern if you examine the roster of the mass-suicide men and women and their leaders. When Jim Jones went down by gunshot after the entire population of his South American cult drank cyanide-laced punch, most of his followers were people whose relatives did not even come forward to provide burial following the tragedy. You can see how someone becomes a cult leader in that tragic shift in which "desire" moves from God to some magical provider!

Both men and women need a network of relationships to maintain moral, mental, and spiritual stability. You can read more about this in the opening chapter of my *Bonding: Relationships in the Image of God.*

6

"Chain of Command":
The Naturalistic Fallacy Goes to Church

We were committed to "family priority," as we understood it, even before we were officially engaged. We have practiced that priority, often imperfectly, for more than fifty years. But our research at Indiana University tossed family issues into my professional lap, and my vocation, since 1969, has been chiefly focused on issues related to the family.[1] In the late sixties, a phenomenon occurred as a popular teacher brought basic teachings about family relationships to every major city throughout the United States. Bill Gothard lectured at his "Institute for Basic Youth Conflicts" with gigantic visuals, making his many points from biblical teaching. In the early seventies, I invited him to come for a teaching lectureship at the seminary where I was beginning my teaching, but his office reported that he was too heavily booked to take school invitations. Eventually, we bought tickets to his seminar at Rupp Arena near us where the University of Kentucky Wildcats play. We commuted to the week-long series.

We were warmed, sometimes confused, by the lecturer's lines of reasoning, but nicely edified in general. We discovered when examining the Scripture indexes he furnished in the syllabus that his best sessions were the ones with the fewest Scripture references. That puzzled us briefly; then we realized that he usually cited dozens of partial verses to prop up a weak idea.

---

[1]Since 1971, we have carried out private research and writing from the Center for the Study of the Family. For a master bibliography, current vita, and travel and speaking schedule contact us by E-mail at: rodojoy@juno.com.

But his best sessions were those that faithfully explored one extended passage in its context.

Then, about midway through the series, the bomb dropped. On the gigantic screen a diagram appeared. It showed a symbol for God, below that a hammer in strike position (the husband) hitting the chisel (the wife), which had sharp and cutting contact with a jewel (their child) that was being shaped. We cringed when the diagram flashed on the screen. The videotaped voice of the fearless leader (by now he had retired from most events and sent only his voice and pictures) invoked a humorous disclaimer for the visual violence suggested by the pictures. But then his serious words plunged us into a grief from which we have not yet recovered:

"Do you know why a husband and a wife cannot have equal authority in the home?" he asked. "It is because 'no man can serve two masters.'"

We were shocked. The implications were enormous. His model inevitably locked marriage and family in conflict, as his seminar title should have warned us. Husband and wife were said to be "competitive adversary masters." What is more, his basic teaching about the family zoomed right past the mystery of "two become one"—past the co-regency of "let them have dominion"—and landed squarely in the territory of sin and curse where the warning sounds: "He shall rule over" the woman (Gen. 3:16). According to this seminar leader, the greatest grief of all human history for Man and Woman was turned into "God's order for families." I worry that this teacher may have committed the unpardonable sin: calling evil good. Robbie and I were grieved to think that so many people were being coached in the historic "Fall model" for marriage and family. We wondered whether to suggest that he rename his family conference, "Basic Youth Conflicts— How to Call Evil Good and Get Away with It."

But we took you to Rupp Arena for quite another reason. As we sat there in the sports gallery, gazing at the video image of the popular family life speaker, a marital fight broke out just two rows in front of us. We had no idea who the distinguished-looking young adults were: two couples were obviously attending the seminar together. The man directly in front of us did some very persistent elbow-to-the-ribs jabs to his wife. He was trying to get her full attention for this "chain of command" image on the screen, as if to tell her that he wanted her to take this point seriously. The woman tried to stand up and leave the row, but he stood up and blocked her, pushing her back down into her seat. Then the woman, in an awkward piece of high stepping, lifted herself out, up, and over the back of her seat and into the empty row between theirs and ours. She sat down alone there, obviously shaken. Her husband then stood up and in an angry whisper to the other couple, said, "Give me your keys. I'll take her out and put her in the car!"

A Naturalistic Fallacy

Suddenly, we realized why we had gone into grief with the speaker's deformed image of husband, wife, and child. He was blind to the actual teaching of Creation, of Jesus, and of St. Paul. He was trying to "baptize" the tragic sin that alienated the first Man and Woman. He was painting a picture of family life that almost exactly matches every pagan culture's view of roles for Man and Woman. It was clear that Bill Gothard was sincere and that he thought he was giving us God's view of the family. We got not a hint that he was aware that his view of male control matched virtually every Stone Age culture in the present world, or that it descended from a line of fallen thinking from which all of us have come. He took a measure of what is and concluded that it *ought to be*. He was naively committing the "naturalistic fallacy" without giving it the slightest thought.

If confronted, Bill Gothard might have said (as another famous family authority said to me), "But I am only teaching what everybody can see is the way that works in every culture of the world." I had cautioned the second lecturer that sin is also universal, and we ought to abandon efforts to salvage the Curse and its consequences by rationalizing that they constitute "God's order for families."

Sociologists have long realized that they must avoid committing the naturalistic fallacy, which holds that *"what is prescribes what ought to be."* They might study sexual behavior in humans and be tempted to declare multiple sexual alliances "normal." But the warning bell, "naturalistic fallacy," goes off. An honest researcher knows to look farther before speaking about what *"ought to be."*

For example, a researcher worked with a thousand couples for ten years in his Problems of Daily Living Clinic at Sinai Hospital in Detroit. He might have reported their sexual histories and then touted: "This is the way couples are supposed to behave." Instead he looked at their life histories and concluded that the pain in the marriages was rooted in their promiscuity. So he avoided the "naturalistic fallacy" and became very helpful to all of us. He observed records of sexual behavior before, outside of, and within the marriages. Only then would he assert: "Sexual intercourse between men and women is constructive only within marriage . . . .Our children should not be having intercourse. We should tell them so. Young adults would have to learn to energize the courtship sequence with feelings, thoughts, and touch rather than coitus. They would then select better partners for better sex that allows a total sexual system commitment."[2] To measure frequency of sexual behavior or sexual tendencies without looking at wider effects is to indulge in that "naturalistic fallacy," justifying certain behavior because it is popular. Perhaps clergy and religious teachers are less careful than sociologists, because they seem likely to "call evil good."

Where the Naturalistic Fallacy Came From

Who defined the naturalistic fallacy? Philosophers David Hume, G. E. Moore, and Bertrand Russell, among others, were the tough-minded "naturalists" who defined and warned against falling into the logical trap declaring *"what is prescribes what ought to be."* One of the most famous of all naturalistic fallacies was an assertion of the Marquis de Sade. He is sometimes referred to as the "father of modern pornography," and he has left his mark in the English language. The term *sadism*, used to describe the violent sexual use of other people, is derived from his name. The Marquis de Sade's fallacy ran like this: *Because the human male is stronger than the human female, males are able to do what they will with females. Therefore, males should use their strength to bring females into compliance with their wishes. Conversely, since women are weaker than men, they should be acquiescent in the face of male demands.* The Marquis de Sade went the next step and declared his observation to be "pure natural determinism." Things *cannot be* any other way, he reasoned, since nature has decreed that men are stronger than women.[3]

It is easy to see how pagans of any sort might indulge in the naturalistic fallacy, but one has to wonder why Christian believers would promote an idea that exploits one group of people by another. In a new church not far from us, the founding pastor guides his staff in a Monday morning meeting about how to handle the guest registrations from the previous day. He asks

---

[2]Paul Pearsall, *Super-Marital Sex: Loving for Life* (New York: Ivy Books, 1987), introduction.

[3]Mark Wade, who was studying with me in the fall of 1984 took an offhand remark and drove it all the way through to construct a summary of the history of the "naturalistic fallacy." Across the decades I have continued to admire his passion for getting things right and checking them out. After a brief career in teaching at the undergraduate level, he has a telecommunications management position in Kansas. I have summarized his findings on the naturalistic fallacy here.

them to place in a temporary file any registration that appears to be from a divorced, single parent, or nonwhite respondent. He is following a strategy to fill his church with white upwardly mobile members—classified as "homogeneous" folks. He may have read the church-growth guidelines that urge such "homogeneous" strategies, even though they are grounded in a naturalistic fallacy. "Follow up with the other guests," he tells his staff, "but we won't be cultivating the temporary file."

It is ironic that "the sons of this world are more shrewd in their generation than the sons of light" (Luke 16:8). Who would have thought that Christians, who have reflected on the bleeding wounds inflicted by hierarchical power everywhere, would be able to ignore the doctrine of Creation and the message of Jesus, announcing instead that this deep flaw in the human race is what *ought to be?*

Checking to Detect the Naturalistic Fallacy

Clearly, *what is* is not necessarily *what ought to be.* Remember these guidelines when someone cites examples of what is and asks you to accept that it *ought to be:*

Get the big picture. When we think, *Everybody is doing it, so it must be okay,* we ought to feel a sort of dizzy discomfort. When we grow accustomed to obscenity, immorality, and deception, we are moving toward indulging in them. The whole culture is slipping into an acceptance that *what is, is what ought to be.* Teen culture is highly vulnerable to buying into the idea that obscene speech, suggestive music lyrics, and pornography are normal. But when we step back and look at cultural patterns that point to decay and the decline of nations and peoples, we can see clearly what comes to such cultures unless they turn away from easy evil.

Keep a fixed point of reference. Existentialism and postmodernity have been popular relativist fads. Existentialism held that each individual creates a personal reality, and that no one else can criticize those individual ideas and values. "Truth" cannot exist, since one person's truth can never be the same as another's truth. Postmodernity observes that each new generation must make up rules as it goes, since one cannot suppose that anything ever set down as truth or right before could apply to today. So everyone must do what is "right in [one's] own eyes" (Deut. 12:8), since there are no fixed rules. Science has provided us with facts, which are offered as a substitute for fixed points of value and belief. The fact-vs.-value chasm in the modern world can be healed by accepting that fixed and unchanging moral and spiritual values can undergird a fact-hungry science. I was young and annoyed when Professor Wilson King punctuated his lectures at Greenville College in 1949 with an assertion, "Nothing is true because it is in the Bible. It is in the Bible because it is true!" I was comfortable with the idea that something was true because it was in the Bible. But Jesus insisted that we should "know the truth" and the truth would "make [us] free" (John 8:32). Jesus said, "I am the way, and the truth, and the life. No one comes to the Father except through me. If you know me, you will know my Father also. From now on you do know him and have seen him" (John 14:6–7, NRSV).

Pay attention to the "three witnesses" to what is true and reliable. Elsewhere[4] I offer more detail, but here is a summary:

1. *Creation:* Take your questions to evidence from the physical world that came from the hand of God. The physical sciences, geology, archeology, and anthropology are just a beginning list of sources. The evidence is no more reliable than the human perceptions and questions that drove the research, but the raw material is straight from the hand of God.

2. *Scripture:* Get deep into Scripture and take it seriously. Scripture addresses every question known to humans. All Scripture is inspired. Scripture is the inspired written record of God's activity in the world. Scripture taken as a whole is entirely reliable and trustworthy. But human interpretation of Scripture is no more reliable than the interpreter.

3. *Jesus:* Most of what we know of Jesus is included in Scripture, but I notice that people who are careful in handling the actual words of Jesus are often less attentive to how He treated people. So again, we must be aware of the perceptions and agendas of anyone who interprets Jesus for us.

We must bring these three witnesses face-to-face with each other. Since Creation, Scripture, and Jesus are all expressions from God, if any of them seems to disagree, we can be sure we are facing a problem of human error. So we need to go back to the baseline again, look over the shoulder of the human interpreter of science, of Scripture, or of Jesus, and sweat over the evidence until all witnesses agree—since they all come from God. This commitment to reconciling the witnesses is the adventure in which each of us is engaged.

---

[4]For my original discussion of these three witnesses, see *Bonding: Relationships in the Image of God* (Nappanee, Ind.: Evangel Publishing House, 1999), pp. 34–37.

A contrast emerges in a fourth witness: degradation and sin. Whatever goes against the affirmations of Creation, Scripture, and Jesus will provide a confirmation of their truth. In Chapter 5 we spread the diagram of history across the page to illustrate how Creation, Fall, and Redemption represent three major epochs by which to take a measure of where we are today in crucial relational issues. Using such a "road map," we then can test the *is* and speculate about whether it might be *ought*. Look at this adaptation of that diagram to locate the trap that gets us into the naturalistic fallacy.

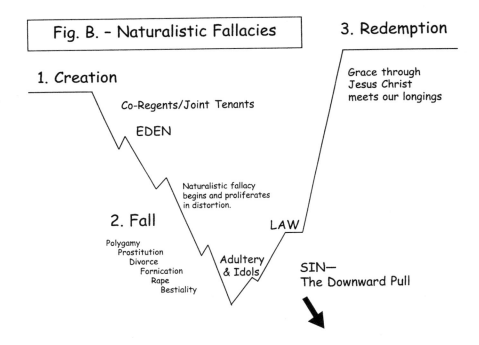

If we could take a sample of human vision, aspiration, or behavior from the period designated as Creation, we might indeed find that it matched *what ought to be.* We can read the first two chapters of Genesis, but if we read them with "fallen eyes," we interpret Paradise through motivations, fears, and biases that are foreign to the innocence reported there. Test points from Creation include these: Is self-interest motivating the behavior? Are the participants indeed innocent? Do the relationships between the man and the woman, or between them and their environment, make for harmony, balance, and ecological well-being? Do their actions take them toward mutual fulfillment, peace, and higher sensitivity to all that is whole, balanced, and harmonious?

But if we based our standards in the chaos that has characterized history since the original sin and degradation occurred, we would find justification for both human relationships and ecological connections that *are* but *should never be*. Here are some test points: Is "progress" for one person or one group at the expense of another? Is behavior motivated by personal profit, gain, or acquisition of power over other people or objects? Does a particular human motivation or behavior lead to mutual wholeness or toward pain, jealousy, arrogance, or destruction? What price and payoff are involved in the transactions? Who is asserting the rights of privilege—those who stand to benefit from the exercise of the rights, or those who stand to pay for them?

Now, try basing our standards in Redemption. Since Jesus, the Second Adam, has shown us what life was meant to be, we will expect to find major perspectives in Redemption that are harmonious with Creation and that contradict human perspectives in Fall and chaos, even when enlightened by Law. Law was a temporary repair, designed to put us back in touch with God's vision for us. But there are problems taking a behavioral sample from the Redemption soil, too.

Redemption denotes the section of the diagram where God's character is written in some people and not in others. So all human relations are carried out in a contaminated moral environment and between "unequals." And, what is even more tricky, God's redemption is at work in various ways in various people. Some respond more authentically to God's character than others. Therefore, a sample of "humans under reconstruction" is not a safe measure of ideal behavior. Some test points might include: Are the relationships mutually enriching and ennobling to everybody involved? Are the implications for everything in the environment positive or destructive? Are there special benefits to any person or group of people, at the expense of another person or group? Is there anything intrinsically demeaning in the sample of behavior? Are the participants transparently honest, open, and holy—the moral equivalent of Creation innocence?

In all of this search it is critical that the three legs of the tripod be firmly shaken down to solid footing: What is implied from Creation (the visible, tangible universe)? What do we learn from Scripture (the amazing account of God's saving design)? And can we see some revealing light in the activity and words of Jesus? These are very likely to turn our lenses toward the highest reality.

Throughout this entire book, we want to look at all of the data, examine and weigh the words and the conceptions from all three witness. So here is our formula: We will anchor the tripod of your microscope on Creation, Scripture, and Jesus. Then we will look for converging evidence among the "witnesses" to evaluate any case of *what is*. For any idea or position that seems to be confirmed by Creation, Scripture, and Jesus, we will cross-reference it against sin and degradation. This reading completes our "universal positioning system."

Why the Chain of Command Works

Two forces keep the "chain of command" working in marriages, families, and corporations: (1) Those who seize control tend to widen their sphere of domination, and (2) the human spirit is corrupted, so it feels "natural" to compete for dominance and control, and to submit to the winner.

Curiously, Scripture nowhere requires women to obey men, though children are required to "obey [their] parents" (Eph. 6:1). "Submission" is commanded everywhere as a requirement of Christian faith and life. "Submit to one another out of reverence for Christ" (Eph. 5:21, NIV) is a principle we will explore in Chapter 8, "Head and Body: The Complete Adam?" It is the grace-based interpersonal strategy for curbing the fallen nature to compete and to dominate others.

Unilateral submission and its partner, unilateral control, present a quiet tragedy. When one person, employee, or spouse "rolls over and plays dead" in passive submission, everyone loses. A successful tyrant in the front office or the home tends to evoke silent rebellion and resentment. But with time, the atrophy of ideas and concerns will yield a bankrupt organization or home. People who do not make decisions and engage in dialogue lose their capacity to think. A woman who is excluded from the command of God to "let them have dominion" (Gen. 1:26) is likely to remain perpetually incompetent. When she finds herself a widow or otherwise alone, she has a steep learning curve to manage her life and that of a household. A man who is dominated by a woman in the same way can become a pitiful waste of potential. Our point here is this: The vertical "chain of command" comes at a very high price. But it "works," especially if what one demands is silence around the house.

In this chapter, we wanted you to ask the question, "Where did we get the 'chain of command' idea for marriage and the family?" We wanted you to consider that it may be a legacy of the Fall, a direct result of disobedience and sin by Woman and Man in Eden, and was never intended as God's order for families. We wanted you to lay out some implications of the popular heresy that *what is, is what ought to be*. If you have begun to do that, then you must be walking with us toward the vision of what God intended for couples. It will take a miracle, of course, if we are to be restored to the image of God, but that is the gracious offer God holds out to us. First He made the Original Adam, then He sent the Second Adam, Jesus. After Jesus, a whole line of re-created Adams is forming. And we are they: man and woman in the image of God. We are going to discover in the final chapter of this book what we are called to become: "The New Adam: From Image to Likeness."

Questions People Ask

Q. *Our pastor teaches the "chain of command" and urges men to "take charge of their wives." I bought into the idea, and "feeling like a lady" was the better part of the arrangement. But I felt very vulnerable, and the arrangement has actually backfired on me. It was hard to imagine that a so-called biblical model could go wrong. But I honestly think it set my husband up to think he was king of the mountain. That mind-set led to his affairs with other women. I could tell I was losing him, and he acted guilty enough, but he would say, "Look at King David and his harem. I'm not that bad!" Eventually, he wanted a divorce. Now I feel really cheated—especially since both of us got our coaching at church. Now I feel that my husband just threw me away.*

A. It is ironic that your church encouraged your husband to inhale a sense of superpower—the "king of the mountain" syndrome. This is the "he shall rule over you" symptom of sin described in Genesis 3. Men are likely to find this "power surge" addictive. Oddly enough, 85 percent of the sixth-day creation species are polygynous, with males presiding over multiple females. Three percent of animals and birds are polyandrous, with slightly larger females dominating a harem of males.[5] John Wesley, in his sermon "On the Brute Creation," insists that human sin sent shock waves throughout the world of animals and birds. Because of human disobedience to God's order, the entire sixth-day creation suffers. Unfortunately, the healing of the species into a peaceable kingdom has to wait for Jesus' return when

---

[5]Compare with Melvin Konner's discussion of variations in "bonding" patterns among the sixth-day creation, including animals and birds, in *The Tangled Wing: Biological Constraints on the Human Spirit* (New York: Holt, Rinehart and Winston, 1982). See the chapter "Lust," pp. 261 ff.

> the wolf shall live with the lamb,
>> the leopard shall lie down with the kid,
> the calf and the lion and the fatling together,
>> and a little child shall lead them. (Isa. 11:6, NRSV)

Men and women, however, are under God's immediate summons to abandon the marks of sin on sex roles and embrace the mystery of "two become one" at a conscious, intentional, and daily obedience level. "Have you not read," Jesus said, in Matthew 19, "that He who made them at the beginning 'made them male and female' . . .?" (v. 4). He went on to add a clincher to the mystery of "two become one" when He said, "Therefore what God has joined together, let not man separate" (Matt. 19:6). Jesus' teaching was all the more striking when we realize that *polygyny* (one man having several wives) was the Jewish norm when Jesus lived, with a limit of six wives per man, except for wealthy or royal males. So Jesus was confronting the male syndrome of pretending to be king of the mountain and trying to take care of several wives. In American culture, this takes the form of a series of affairs or a series of wives.

Ironically, while some Christian teachers and ministers advocate the "chain of command" as God's order for couples, that model may make marriage partners more vulnerable to abuse. James M. Alsdurf studied the ways pastors advise women who report physical abuse from their husbands. He found that pastors in rigidly conservative traditions not only advised women to accept physical and emotional abuse in marriage, but often sent them back into the abusive environment, believing that Scripture justifies men's abusing women.[6]

You can see how urgent it is for both men and women to dig into Scripture for themselves and to find communities of faith that distinguish between God's design and destructive concepts grounded in sin and negative consequences. You were wounded in a church that likely was naive in its bad teaching, but you are bearing real consequences and deserve the care and support of a biblically well-grounded church.

---

[6]James Alsdurf reports in *Wife Abuse and Christian Faith: An Assessment of the Church's Response* (Pasadena: Fuller Theological Seminary, 1985). See also James and Phyllis Alsdurf, *Battered into Submission* (Colorado Springs: InterVarsity Press, 1989). In this book, the husband-and-wife team explore biblical and theological questions in the light of Dr. Alsdurf's research at Fuller.

We should note, too, that some new Christians are damaged by their churches' teaching about Christian discipline, which leads them to do violent things to their children. You can count on it: Violence in relationships is always rooted in sin and evil, not in God.

Q. *Are you the only people challenging the idea that women always submit to men?*

A. Not at all. In fact, I made a point of checking in with Promise Keepers early in its start-up. In 1994, I flew to Denver just to participate in this amazing men's movement. Dr. Chuck Swindoll, then newly named president of Dallas Seminary, was a keynote speaker. After riding in on a Harley motorcycle, trailing a dozen or more converted bikers, he mounted the podium and began by saying he wanted to speak from the Ephesians material on "submission." But first he wanted to repeat a story told by Pastor Jack Hayford two years before from the Boulder platform. The story told of a couple who attended a seminar about family relationships where the "chain of command" was being taught. At seeing the diagram about a husband's "responsibility" to take charge, the young man inhaled deeply and whispered to his wife, "This is the first day of a new marriage for us!" His wife looked the other way. In the car, headed home late that night, he repeated his energized affirmation. She looked out the other side of the car. But after driving into their garage and entering the kitchen of their home, the husband stopped his wife, took her by her shoulders, backed her against the refrigerator, and said, "Look at me. This is the first day of a marriage in which I'm taking charge." Swindoll said it was about three days before he saw his wife again. Then, very slowly, he began to see her out of one eye.

Sixty thousand men roared with the joke Swindoll had pulled. He moved quickly into the submission teachings in Ephesians. Then he made a painful confession: "We have suffered many things at the hands of people who have done a lot of bad teaching from this passage. If anybody needs to comment on the verse that says wives submit to their husbands, I leave it to them. But today I want to spend my entire time with you telling you what it means for a husband to submit to his wife."

I turned to sweep the stadium with my gaze and prayed Simeon's prayer: *If the president of Dallas Seminary is correcting the distortions that have abused us all, "Lord, let your servant depart in peace! I'm no longer needed on this planet."*

There are notable places where you can turn for help in getting Man and Woman teachings grounded in both Creation and gospel. Willow Creek Community Church, Barrington, IL, is one of the great congregations where the careful research and teaching on sex roles have come down carefully and well. Both *Beyond Sex Roles* and *Community 101* come out of Willow Creek research and writing by Pastor Bill Hybels' mentor, Dr. Gilbert Bilezikian.[7]

Christians for Biblical Equality provides teaching events and lists of resources that are sensitized to the sovereignty of Man and Woman established in Creation. The organization is in the best tradition of conservative biblical scholarship and practice.[8]

---

[7]We found the report on the Willow Creek Church research in Gilbert Bilezikian, *Beyond Sex Roles: A Guide for the Study of Female Roles in the Bible* (Grand Rapids: Baker, 1985). See also his *Community 101: Reclaiming the Local Church as the Community of Oneness* (Grand Rapids: Zondervan, 1997).

[8]Christians for Biblical Equality sponsors conventions and pursues conversations grounding human relationships in scriptural teaching. You can reach them easily at the office of the executive director by E-mail: cbe@cbeinternational.org. They maintain offices in Minneapolis.

7

On Silencing Women in the Church

Julia Arnold Shelhamer was a legend in our church circles long before we actually met her. Then she moved from Washington, D.C., to "retire" at Winona Lake, Indiana, where we lived and worked. That was in the late 1960s, and she must have been in her eighties.

"How do you like living at Winona Lake?" Dr. J. F. Gregory, another long-term denominational leader, asked her one day after she arrived.

"Very well," she said, "but I miss the drunks." Julia answered casually. Her mission to the underclass was widely known and respected. Julia took the honors for originating Dial-A-Prayer. The ministry began with her phone number, where she listened, counseled, and prayed with the anonymous people who called.

Mrs. Shelhamer later moved to Wilmore, Kentucky, because her daughter, Esther James, wanted her mother living nearby. So we followed Julia Shelhamer's adventures in Kentucky. She hired a seminary student to take her to Keene, Kentucky, for a few hours each week, where she taught elocution to African-American children.

Julia was a world-class woman. On her ninety-sixth birthday, she spoke in chapel at Oakdale Christian High School in Breathitt County, long a favorite school of hers. About two years earlier, Julia preached a ten-day revival in Watts, Los Angeles.

Esther James, her daughter, today carries on much of the spirit and witness of her mother. She wrote about her mother in *Daughters of Sarah* magazine:

At the age of thirteen Julia was impressed with God's call to Jeremiah in chapter one, and felt that verses 4–9 applied also to her. Since helping to bring people into a right relationship with God was the only important business of life, every available evening was spent attending revivals or assisting in street meetings in Chicago's saloon and red light districts. At seventeen she was asked to speak every Wednesday night to large numbers of derelict men at Olive Branch Mission, and before her marriage at twenty-three she had received calls to assist in revivals in several Illinois churches.

At about eighteen she was prevented from receiving an evangelist's license from a certain official board by a leading board member's loud denunciation of women preachers. Naturally she keenly felt the rejection, even though she had not asked for the license. Her friends then went through other legal channels and secured for her a license from the district quarterly conference. Much later in life, after preaching in nearly every state and on two missionary trips around the world, she was ordained deacon. She [Julia] says,

"A few times in my life we have met men who openly and strenuously opposed the idea of a woman preaching the Gospel. This once greatly troubled my reticent spirit, but I have learned to go right on as though there were no opposition. Time is too short and God's work too important to stop and parley with opposers. I notice that such men are doing little if anything toward aggressive evangelism. It is not my business to offer an apology to them for the commission given to me by the King."[1]

Another biographer, Glen Williamson, wrote of Julia:

Through the greater part of a century, [Julia] would give herself without reservation to the physical and spiritual welfare of others—a tiny enthusiastic woman, who twice

---

[1] Esther James, "Our Foremothers: Julia Arnold Shelhamer," *Daughters of Sarah*, November-December 1981, pp. 10–11.

would encircle the globe with the gospel, raise hundreds of thousands of dollars for the underprivileged, be invited up from her little mission to sit at breakfast with the President of the United States, and whose remarkable ministry among the suffering would be featured in *Time* magazine. And greater than these things, her humility and simple faith in God could not be destroyed.

Williamson documented her preaching style:

Without yelling she made them hear; without weeping she brought tears to the eyes of wicked, wretched men; without resorting to any of the tricks of the professions she invited sinners to the altar, and they came, weeping, repenting, believing, and were saved. [2]

Julia's life demonstrated that God gives extraordinary gifts to women as well as men. God calls women to leadership, just as He calls men. Our relationships and our world will be much richer if we recognize this.

Doesn't Everybody Agree?

Many societies (including American society until recent years) have assumed that women are supposed to be controlled by men. Tragically, some Christians accept this distorted and erroneous misunderstanding of their culture as being right, and do not bother to look carefully at the Scripture.

Little Scripture knowledge can be dangerous. By way of illustration, let's string together the proof texts that are commonly used to "prove" that men ought to control women:

I want you to know that the head of every man is Christ, the head of woman is man, and the head of Christ is God. (1 Cor. 11:3)

[34]. . . Women should remain silent in the churches. They are not allowed to speak, but must be in submission, as the Law says. [35]If they want to inquire about something, they should

---

[2]Glen Williamson, *Julia: Giantess in Controversy* (Indianapolis: Light and Life Press, 1969), pp. 15, 50.

ask their own husbands at home; for it is disgraceful for a woman to speak in the church. (1 Cor. 14:34–35, NIV)

²²Wives, submit to your husbands as to the Lord. ²³For the husband is the head of the wife as Christ is the head of the church, his body, of which he is the Savior. ²⁴Now as the church submits to Christ, so also wives should submit to their husbands in everything. (Eph. 5:22–24, NIV)

¹¹A woman should learn in quietness and full submission. ¹²I do not permit a woman to teach or to have authority over a man; she must be silent. ¹³For Adam was formed first, then Eve. ¹⁴And Adam was not the one deceived; it was the woman who was deceived and became a sinner. ¹⁵But women will be saved through childbearing—if they continue in faith, love and holiness with propriety. (1 Tim. 2:11–15, NIV)

³Likewise, teach the older women to be reverent in the way they live, not to be slanderers or addicted to much wine, but to teach what is good. ⁴Then they can train the younger women to love their husbands and children, ⁵to be self-controlled and pure, to be busy at home, to be kind, and to be subject to their husbands, so that no one will malign the word of God. (Titus 2:3–5, NIV)

¹Wives, in the same way be submissive to your husbands so that, if any of them do not believe the word, they may be won over without words by the behavior of their wives, ²when they see the purity and reverence of your lives....⁵For this is the way the holy women of the past who put their hope in God used to make themselves beautiful. They were submissive to their own husbands, ⁶like Sarah, who obeyed Abraham and called him her master. You are her daughters if you do what is right and do not give way to fear. (1 Pet. 3:1–2, 5-6, NIV)

To the woman he [the Lord God] said,
    "I will greatly increase your pains in childbearing;
    with pain you will give birth to children.

> Your desire will be for your husband,
>> and he will rule over you." (Gen. 3:16, NIV)

Here we have in twenty-two verses the core of the argument to demand that women submit to men. If we isolate the verses from their larger contexts and string them like pearls, we can see the grim pattern: Women are to regard men as their "head." Women are always to submit to men. Women are to be silent in the church. Women are to teach women, never men. They are to stay at home, to obey and be ruled over by men.

Now let's review these texts more carefully, both to put them in context and to reconcile them with other writings from the same authors. Scripture must be interpreted within the "big picture" and reconciled within this ultimate context of what is biblical.

Is the "Curse" God's Will for Women?

Let's begin with, Genesis 3, the painful story of sin and its consequences. Only two specific "curses" are announced: God's curse on the serpent and curse on the soil. But consequences are detailed for both the woman and the man. The consequences to the woman are painful patterns that will haunt all of her relationships—in the conception and delivery of her children, and in her relationship to her husband:

> To the woman he [the Lord God] said,
>> "I will greatly increase your pains in childbearing;
>> with pain you will give birth to children.
> Your desire will be for your husband,
>> and he will rule over you" (Gen. 3:16, NIV).

The consequences of sin have their greatest impact on man with regard to his vocation. No longer does he tend the delightful Garden in quiet companionship with God, but

> In the sweat of your face you shall eat bread
> Till you return to the ground,
> For out of it you were taken;
> For dust you *are*,
> And to dust you shall return" (Gen. 3:19).

In neither case are the sinful humans "cursed" by God. We could argue that these foreboding words are descriptive of the consequences of their sin, rather than prescriptive of God's condemnation of their sin. Remember that the warning against eating from the "tree of the knowledge of good and evil" was stated in Genesis 2:16–17: "You may freely eat of every tree of the garden; but of the tree of the knowledge of good and evil you shall not eat, for in the day that you eat of it you shall die" (NRSV). This "knowing" denoted discovery through painful experience, in contrast with accepting God's wisdom. The man's and the woman's rejection of God's wisdom led them and their offspring into the self-chosen way of suffering and death.

Peter and Paul: New Testament Principles

We have anchor points for understanding God's plan for couples in Genesis and Revelation, both of which describe a "bride and groom." And it is clear that the primary concept of "two become one" applies to both sets of bride and groom, plus all monogamous couples under the blessing of Jesus in Matthew 19: "So they are no longer two, but one flesh. Therefore what God has joined together, let no one separate" (v. 6, NRSV). We are obligated to interpret all of Scripture in a way that affirms this consistent conceptual standard. So when we study the writings of Peter and Paul, we should expect that neither will contradict the "two become one" principle, and the Creation affirmation, "Let them have dominion."

Peter states on the Day of Pentecost:

> [14]Fellow Jews and all of you who live in Jerusalem, let me explain this to you; listen carefully to what I say. [15]These men are not drunk, as you suppose. It's only nine in the morning! [16]No this is what was spoken by the prophet Joel:
>
> > [17]"In the last days, God says,
> > I will pour out my Spirit on all people.
> > Your sons and daughters will prophesy,
> >   your young men will see visions,
> >   your old men will dream dreams.
> > [18]Even on my servants, both men and women,
> >   I will pour out my Spirit in those days,
> >   and they will prophesy.
> > [19]I will show wonders in the heaven above

and signs on the earth below,
blood and fire and billows of smoke.
    The sun will be turned to darkness
and the moon to blood
before the coming of the great and
    glorious day of the Lord.
[21]And everyone who calls on the name of the Lord
    will be saved." (Acts 2:14–21, NIV)

Here Peter picks up the Creation vision for humankind and announces it as Redemption's vision. He uses the words of the prophet Joel (Joel 2:28–32) to announce the persistent will of God:

1. *All people:* Traditional racial and ethnic distinctions are ended.

2. *Sons and daughters prophesy:* Sex distinctions are erased.

3. *Young and old:* Age discrimination is abolished.

4. *Men and women* (literally, "maid servants" and "men servants"). Social and gender distinctions are irrelevant.

Paul establishes his perspective on men and women in his epistle to the Galatians, and all of his teachings must be brought home to this baseline:

[26]You are all sons of God through faith in Christ Jesus, [27]for all of you who were baptized into Christ have clothed yourselves with Christ. [28]There is neither Jew nor Greek, slave nor free, male nor female, for you are all one in Christ Jesus. [29]If you belong to Christ, then you are Abraham's seed, and heirs according to the promise. (Gal. 3:26–29, NIV)

Here Paul joins Peter in detailing the transformations that are to be expected in the Christian community:

1. *Neither Jew nor Greek:* Racial differences are abolished.

2. *Neither slave nor free:* Social, political, economic, and class differences are erased.

3. *Neither male nor female:* Inequality based on gender is ended.

Submission—Tracing the Teachings

With these sweeping general rules from both Peter and Paul so clearly stated, we must resist making any sweeping contradictory rule out of any other statement from either Peter or Paul. We should bring apparent contradictions to these foundational utterances and ask how we might interpret each seeming contradiction in the light of the Creation-Redemption baselines here. Let's begin with Peter's writing in his first epistle:

> ¹Wives, in the same way be submissive to your husbands so that, if any of them do not believe the word, they may be won over without words by the behavior of their wives, ²when they see the purity and reverence of your lives. . . . ⁵For this is the way the holy women of the past who put their hope in God used to make themselves beautiful. They were submissive to their own husbands, ⁶like Sarah, who obeyed Abraham and called him her master. You are her daughters if you do what is right and do not give way to fear. (1 Pet. 3:1-2, 5-6, NIV)

Before we become preoccupied with the phrase about "wives" being "submissive," it is worth asking what Peter may be referring to when he says "in the same way." This phrase refers back to the case of Jesus, who suffered for doing good and endured it: "When they hurled their insults at him, he did not retaliate; when he suffered, he made no threats. Instead, he entrusted himself to him who judges justly" (1 Pet. 2:23, NIV). The case of Jesus becomes Peter's hallmark to illustrate a Christian principle to guide in relating to "every authority instituted among men: whether to the king...or to governors. . . . For it is God's will that by doing good you should silence the ignorant talk of foolish men. . . . Show proper respect to everyone: Love the brotherhood of believers, fear God, honor the King" (1 Pet. 2:13–17, NIV).

"In the same way" may also refer to the predicament of slaves: "Slaves, submit yourselves to your masters with all respect, not only to those who are good and considerate, but also to those who are harsh" (1 Pet. 2:18, NIV). So Peter draws "the worst case," then advises women in the Christian community who may be receiving the "worst treatment" to follow the example of loyal slaves. In Peter's congregations, as in many of ours, abused women needed comfort, support, and special teaching to help them cope with a spiritually fractured household. Peter's advice to such women suggests how, unilaterally, they might "make a difference" by practicing the general policy of submission. Clearly, this message was addressed to women with unbelieving husbands. It was the Christian woman's secret strategy, offered by her counselor and spiritual advisor, Peter.

Ironically, husbands get the final treatment in Peter's series of exhortations to behave "in the same way." Look back into 1 Peter 2 and trace the sequence. Notice that each is an instance of a set of relationships in a broken world. Repeatedly, Peter advises that submission is effective as a way to live faithfully in relationships. All people should submit to kings. Slaves should submit to masters. Wives should submit to husbands. Then comes a warning: All of this is done "in the same way" that Jesus submitted to torture and death. Husbands should exalt their wives and affirm the "two become one," lest their prayers not be answered. Look at the text: "Husbands, in the same way be considerate as you live with your wives, and treat them with respect as the weaker partner and as heirs with you of the gracious gift of life, so that nothing will hinder your prayers" (1 Pet. 3:7, NIV).

The husbands have been included in Peter's orders to submit to kings and to those who abuse them. But something here is added, and it is a vision right out of creation. In the beginning, man and woman were co-regents. Each was charged with "dominion," as joint tenants of the planet. Now, Peter reminds the couple that they are joint heirs of the gracious gift of God's redeeming new life. A husband and a wife are challenged to prove the sincerity of their commitment, showing how "two become one." Self-centered human beings persistently drift toward arrogance and exclusion, but faith requires us to dance the dance of respect and unity. All of Peter's teaching is couched in the language of mutual consideration and mutual respect. He alludes to the man's protecting his mate with his musculature, but also to their equality, being bathed in God's grace. Peter's brief advice to husbands closes with the caution to be careful in this marital relationship, "so that nothing will hinder your prayers." Is this a magic formula for the man to get his prayers answered? Likely not. But imagine how gentle all good men might be, if we realized that our moral and spiritual character is subject to the acid test of evaluating how we treat our wives.

When I was invited to visit the maximum security Orient Prison in the Ohio State Penitentiary system, where Chaplain Don York had coached several dozen men through my book, *Men Under Construction*, the prisoners demanded that Robbie accompany me to a talkback session. The prisoners insisted that, if they could watch Robbie, they would know whether I was telling the truth as I responded to their tough questions! We had a glorious afternoon at Orient Prison, and the men gladly received both my responses and Robbie's active participation in the dialogue!

Paul, writing to Titus who is "left behind" in Crete, outlines a primer of behavioral standards for new believers in that pagan culture. It includes some submission challenges, so read it carefully from Titus1:5–3:11. This passage gives us a sense of the culture of Paul's day, as the apostle offers Titus a list of behavioral standards for the new Christians. Note that his major worry is that the new Christian believers on the island of Crete will be overly influenced by "Jewish myths" and "those who reject the truth." [3]

Look at Paul's unvarnished description of Cretans in 1:12. Although this is a private letter to Titus, we cringe at Paul's candid and pessimistic view of Cretans. It doesn't sound either politically correct or kind. What kind of ministry works with people like the Cretans, whose boundaries are battered down and whose hopes are shattered? Paul says Titus must begin a program of intentional discipleship.

So read this entire text again and again with the "challenge to culture" that Paul is wise to see. If these Cretans "become sound in the faith," then the Christian must hold out to them a set of behaviors that is "consistent with sound doctrine."

Note the sequence of populations Paul targets: older men, older women, younger men. (Nothing is said about younger women, except that "older women" are to be their teachers.) Paul knows the power of "generational sin and generational grace." We are often less attentive to this pattern. If you want to see a child or a teen converted to Christ, begin evangelizing that kid's grandparents.

In this emerging "conversion culture" on the island of Crete, Paul wisely focuses on the influence of godly, mature men. When my great-grandson Tyler, at age four, picks up the heavy earpiece of the antique phone next to my digital phone as I am talking on business, he repeats my exact phrases and my inflection. He is literally inventing a school for learning "how to do a man's work and how to talk manly talk." Likewise, when he wants a cap like

---

[3]As an interesting side issue about marriage, note that the NRSV struggles with "husband of one wife," which is the more common translation of the phrase in 1:6, giving us the paraphrase, "married only once." Yet the standard Paul asserts is clearly an insistence on exclusive monogamy expressed in a culture in which Jewish men of wealth could have up to six wives simultaneously. That was true in the Palestine of Jesus' day, as Josephus reports. It is not easy for us to read "husband of one wife" without thinking it demands an all-male clergy. But remember the principle I have offered you: Be sure you reconcile "Paul with Paul" before you take an isolated phrase and impose it on all time and overpower all other Scriptures.

I wear while working and asks for a tool like mine to help me, he is mimicking adult ways.

Paul knows the social patterns by which men "hang out" together and are vulnerable to one another's degenerative talk. Robbie and I occasionally grab breakfast at a McDonald's restaurant that at breakfast time seems always to be nicely populated with retired men. They consistently occupy the same fifteen or twenty nonsmoking places, and their banter is wonderfully serious talk, laced with stories and humor. For example, in one sitting, we overheard their conversations about a pastor who was in trouble and was having to leave the community. They talked about people who are fighting cancer and how they hoped they will beat it. Imagine the power of cultivating older men to talk seriously about their own and other people's needs, to devise strategies for solving health, financial, and social problems that rip through every community. Look at the character criteria of "older men" and in Paul's advice to Titus, celebrate Paul's wisdom.

"Older women" are vulnerable in Crete (and perhaps elsewhere) to gossiping slander, and to abuse of drugs and alcohol. They need to be challenged to rise to the higher calling of overcoming evil with good. They are to teach the next generation what is good. That assertion seems not to be exclusively limited to teaching the "younger women." Yet the older women's teaching can empower younger women who regard them as models, demonstrating how to love their husbands and their children, and showing how to be "chaste, good managers of the household, [and] kind."

For a moment, I want you to look carefully at the list of recommended behaviors without racing to the final statement that younger women should be "submissive to their husbands." All of these items are crucial "so that the word of God may not be discredited."

Following "older women," Paul turns to tell Titus to "urge the younger men to be self-controlled." Cretan young men were evidently much like each generation of young men where you and I live: They think most of the time about how to get what they want and how to get it quickly. Paul urges Titus to adopt the mentor role for these younger men. Youth ministers tend to get stuck in their own delayed youthful adolescence, and they fail to challenge the young men and women. Don't you wish every youth minister would post this text on his or her mirror to shape every day's personal behavior? "Show yourself in all respects a model of good works, and in your teaching show integrity, gravity, and sound speech that cannot be censured; then any opponent will be put to shame, having nothing evil to say of us" (Tit. 2:7–8,

NRSV). Young men need mentors who are adult in every way. So between Titus' s mentoring and the high integrity pattern they will see in the "older men," even the young men of Crete can know the transforming work of God's grace.

"Tell slaves to be submissive to their masters" (Titus 2:9, NRSV). Here Paul goes to some length detailing what a Christian slave (or employee?) should do. Slowly read and reread 2:11–3:11 and let the description of godly, holy living pour over you like a transforming baptism of God's grace. The burden of Paul in this passage is for gracious and empowered Christian integrity. Also note the caution in 3:9 about avoiding "stupid controversies, genealogies, dissensions, and quarrels about the law" (NRSV). Much of the debate about women's roles and responsibilities in the church likely violates these warnings.

The principles in both Titus and 1 Peter are simple and profound: (1) Show respect/reverence all around. (2) Teach those younger than you, especially those who are likely to be going over the same life curriculum as you—i.e., those of the same sex and probable cultural influences. Finally, (3) remember that servanthood and submission are always the marks of a Christian. Always try nonresistance and graciousness in an effort to de-escalate a conflict and to establish a peaceable relationship. Only when violence and persistent abuse continue, something else kicks in: "After a first and second admonition, have nothing more to do with anyone who causes divisions, since you know that such a person is perverted and sinful, being self-condemned" (Titus 3:10–11, NRSV). So Paul is not soft on the "liars, vicious brutes, lazy gluttons" that were the norm in Cretan society. With Paul's high sense of moral outrage, do not imagine that he would send a woman or a man back to a persistently abusing spouse, or children back into a persistently humiliating and abusing home.

On Submitting to One Another

I reported Chuck Swindoll's self-control at the Promise Keepers meeting in Boulder, Colorado, when he said that he wanted to talk about how men should submit to women. His distinction was in the spirit of Paul. Men need to attend first of all to their own obedience to Jesus. Women need to feel the sting of rebuke that applies specifically to women. If we agreed to pay attention to Jesus and mind our own business, we would all find higher ground in our walk with God. Remember the Jesus formula:

Why do you see the speck in your neighbor's eye, but do not notice the log in your own eye? Or how can you say to your neighbor, "Let me take the speck out of your eye," while the log is in your own eye? You hypocrite, first take the log out of your own eye, and then you will see clearly to take the speck out of your neighbor's eye. (Matt. 7:3–5, NRSV)

Now look at the most often quoted teaching on submission, Ephesians 5:15–6:9. It is not especially about submission (which we tend to grab for obvious "power" reasons) but about characteristics of all of us who live in days that "are evil." If we are "filled with the Spirit," Paul says we will have certain characteristics. Compare the NRSV text with NASB and NIV. The italics that appear in verse 22 in the NASB show that there is no verb following the word "wives." It is implied from verse 21. However, verse 21 says submission is universally required of those "filled with the spirit." The text climaxes in verse 31, by returning to Creation—where the mystery is that Man and Woman "become one."

> [15]Therefore be careful how you walk, not as unwise men but as wise, [16]making the most of your time, because the days are evil. [17]So then do not be foolish, but understand what the will of the Lord is. [18]And do not get drunk with wine, for that is dissipation, but be filled with the Spirit, [19]speaking to one another in psalms and hymns and spiritual songs, singing and making melody with your heart to the Lord; [20]always giving thanks for all things in the name of our Lord Jesus Christ, even the Father; [21]and be subject to one another in the fear of Christ.

> [22]Wives, be *subject* to your own husbands, as unto the Lord. [23]For the husband is the head of the wife, as Christ also is the head of the church, He Himself *being* the Savior of the body. [24]But as the church is subject to Christ, so also the wives *ought to be* to their husbands in everything.

> [25]Husbands, love your wives, just as Christ also loved the church and gave Himself up for her, [26]so that He might sanctify her, having cleansed her by the washing of water with the word, [27]that He might present to Himself the church in all her

glory, having no spot or wrinkle or any such thing; but that she would be holy and blameless. [28]So husbands ought also to love their own wives as their own bodies. He who loves his own wife loves himself; [29]for no one ever hated his own flesh, but nourishes and cherishes it, just as Christ also does the church, [30]because we are members of His body. [31]FOR THIS REASON A MAN SHALL LEAVE HIS FATHER AND MOTHER AND SHALL BE JOINED TO HIS WIFE, AND THE TWO SHALL BECOME ONE FLESH. [32]This mystery is great; but I am speaking with reference to Christ and the church. [33]Nevertheless, each individual among you also is to love his own wife even as himself, and the wife must see to it that she respects her husband. [1]Children, obey your parents in the Lord, for this is right. [2]HONOR YOUR FATHER AND MOTHER (which is the first commandment with a promise), [3]SO THAT IT MAY BE WELL WITH YOU, AND THAT YOU MAY LIVE LONG ON THE EARTH.

[4]Fathers, do not provoke your children to anger, but bring them up in the discipline and instruction of the Lord.

[5]Slaves, be obedient to those who are your masters according to the flesh, with fear and trembling, in the sincerity of your heart, as to Christ; [6]not by way of eyeservice, as men-pleasers, but as slaves of Christ, doing the will of God from the heart. [7]With good will render service, as to the Lord, and not to men, [8]knowing that whatever good thing each one does, this he will receive back from the Lord, whether slave or free.

[9]And masters, do the same things to them, and give up threatening, knowing that both their Master and yours is in heaven, and there is no partiality with Him.

(Eph. 5:15–6:9, NASB)

Count the number of times *head* appears in 5:22–30. Now count the number of times *body* appears. Given the difference in frequency (*head*, 2; *body* or *bodies*, 3), why would teachers and preachers be so preoccupied with making assertions about "headship?" Why haven't speakers stressed "bodyship"?

As in the Titus passage, the range of relationships and responsibilities extends beyond husband and wife, and teaches about slaves. The grim truth is that slave owners must know, if they are Spirit filled, "that both their Master and yours is in heaven, and there is no partiality with Him (6:9, NASB). The added material here on children's obedience to parents is nicely balanced with caution to fathers not to provoke their children to anger, but to "bring them up in the discipline and instruction of the Lord" (6:4, NASB).

So that we will have full coverage of Paul's "submission" teachings, look at a parallel passage in Colossians 3–4. Notice that 3:10 describes the painful past from which the Colossian believers have been delivered—with a list of tragic life patterns that looks almost as hopeless as that of the Cretans. These verses follow:

> [11]In that renewal there is no longer Greek and Jew, circumcised and uncircumcised, barbarian, Scythian, slave and free; but Christ is all and in all!
>
> [12]As God's chosen ones, holy and beloved, clothe yourselves with compassion, kindness, humility, meekness, and patience. [13]Bear with one another and, if anyone has a complaint against another, forgive each other; just as the Lord has forgiven you, so you also must forgive. [14]Above all, clothe yourselves with love, which binds everything together in perfect harmony. [15]And let the peace of Christ rule in your hearts, to which indeed you were called in the one body. And be thankful. [16]Let the word of Christ dwell in you richly; teach and admonish one another in all wisdom; and with gratitude in your hearts sing psalms, hymns, and spiritual songs to God. [17]And whatever you do, in word or deed, do everything in the name of the Lord Jesus, giving thanks to God the Father through him.
>
> [18]Wives, be subject to your husbands, as is fitting in the Lord. [19]Husbands, love your wives, and never treat them harshly. [20]Children, obey your parents in everything, for this is your acceptable duty in the Lord. [21]Fathers, do not provoke your children, or they may lose heart. [22]Slaves, obey your earthly masters in everything, not only while being watched and in

order to please them, but wholeheartedly, fearing the Lord. [23]Whatever your task, put yourselves into it, as done for the Lord and not for your masters, [24]since you know that from the Lord you will receive the inheritance as your reward: you serve the Lord Christ. [25]For the wrongdoer will be paid back for whatever wrong has been done, and there is no partiality.

[1]Masters, treat your slaves justly and fairly, for you know that you also have a Master in heaven. (Col. 3:11–4:1, NRSV)

The whole text appeals to transformation through love, and to gentleness in all relationships. The Apostle's advice applies to wives, husbands, children, fathers, and masters (employers?). So how shortsighted it is to focus our attention on one phrase and to make it a "law of the church" to discriminate against wives and other women!

Taken together, such passages on "submitting to one another out of reverence for Christ" apply to everyone who lives in obedience to Jesus and walks in the power of God's Spirit. These include:

- Wives submit to their husbands.

- Husbands submit by laying down their lives to protect their wives.

- Children submit by obeying their parents.

- Fathers submit by not exasperating their children.

- Slaves (employees?) submit by being honest and working diligently, even when not being watched.

- Masters (employers?) submit by being gentle and fair, remembering that God is both their own Master and Master of the slaves, and "there is no partiality" with God.

This is a sort of "dance of service and gracious deference" played out by equals under the loving eye of the Creator who loves us all the same. Submission is a Christian obligation not assigned to women alone. No special class, gender, or status group is eligible for exclusion from the command.

Look now at another passage from Paul, recorded in 1 Corinthians 11:2-16. Here is that word for "head" again. The actual Greek word is *kephale* (literally, the anatomical "head"). We will look at this passage further in Chapter 10, "'Head': Another Name for Husbands?":

> ²I commend you because you remember me in everything and maintain the traditions just as I handed them on to you. ³But I want you to understand that Christ is the head of every man, and the husband is the head of his wife, and God is the head of Christ. ⁴Any man who prays or prophesies with something on his head disgraces his head, ⁵but any woman who prays or prophesies with her head unveiled disgraces her head—it is one and the same thing as having her head shaved. ⁶For if a woman will not veil herself, then she should cut off her hair; but if it is disgraceful for a woman to have her hair cut off or to be shaved, she should wear a veil. ⁷For a man ought not to have his head veiled, since he is the image and reflection of God; but woman is the reflection of man. ⁸Indeed, man was not made from woman, but woman from man. ⁹Neither was man created for the sake of woman, but woman for the sake of man. ¹⁰For this reason a woman ought to have a symbol of authority on her head, because of the angels. ¹¹Nevertheless, in the Lord woman is not independent of man or man independent of woman. ¹²For just as woman came from the man, so man comes through woman; but all things come from God. ¹³Judge for yourselves: is it proper for a woman to pray to God with her head unveiled? ¹⁴Does not nature itself teach you that if a man wears long hair, it is degrading to him, ¹⁵but if a woman has long hair, it is her glory? For her hair is given to her for a covering. ¹⁶But if anyone is disposed to be contentious— we have no such custom, nor do the churches of God. (1 Cor. 11:2-16, NRSV)

Look now at another passage from Paul, recorded in 1 Corinthians 11:2–16. Here is that word for "head" again. The Greek word is *kephale* (literally, the anatomical "head"). We will look at the passage further in Chapter 10, "'Head'—Another Name for Husbands?" Here are complicated teachings about what is appropriate hair management, head covering, and how men and women reflect different aspects of "the image," and where the symbols of authority are for men and for women. In 11:12, as if Paul sensed he might be segregating men and women into some hierarchical pattern, he asserts: "Just as woman came from man, so man comes through woman; but all things come from God" (NRSV). The bottom line is that the "churches of God" will not tolerate conflict over such things.

Silencing Women in Church

We now want to consider two passages that seem, in isolation, to close the door on women's having any vocal leadership in the church.[4] If 1 Timothy 2:11–15 were to become the top-ranking theological statement about women in the church, it would also have to be the top statement about sin and salvation. We then would be stuck with a strange cultic profile: Women are sinners; men are not. Women need salvation; they get it by bearing children. Such an assertion would be enough to silence women in the church and keep them working for unlimited conceptions and deliveries as a means for their eternal salvation.

Therefore, if we make this a normative doctrinal passage, it stands in shocking contrast to two clear teachings about sin and salvation everywhere named in Scripture: (1) There is gender solidarity in the first sin; both Man and Woman were disobedient and came under consequences of their decisions. (2) Salvation is through faith alone in Jesus.

But Paul is transparently clear here: Women are both to learn in quietness and to be silent. Is there any other way to say it? Paul thinks of a way: "I do not permit a woman to teach or to have authority over a man."

> [11]A woman should learn in quietness and full submission. [12]I do not permit a woman to teach or to have authority over a man; she must be silent. [13]For Adam was formed first, then Eve. [14]And Adam was not the one deceived; it was the woman who was deceived and became a sinner. [15]But women will be saved through childbearing—if they continue in faith, love and holiness with propriety. (1 Tim. 2:11-15, NIV)

---

[4]Notice that in 1 Corinthians 11:5, where hair styles and head covering are in focus, Paul assumes that women will be praying and preaching/prophesying in public.

[5]For example, see Berkeley Mickelson "Women in the Church," a paper presented at the Baptist General Conference, Spring 1980. See also Robert Rood Moore, "Dilemma of Interpretation: Illustrated by Paul's View of the Role of Women in the Church" (Asbury College, Wilmore, Kentucky, ca. 1982).

Biblical scholars and interpreters have made several attempts to resolve the problem. Is this a specific teaching addressing a specific problem and not a universal rule?[5] Is it a temporary "order" designed to keep the teaching channel open to prepared and wise teachers, in an environment plagued by heresy and the abuse of incompetent teachers.[6] Does the key to the passage lie in the unusual Greek word translated "have authority over?"

In looking at the word translated "have authority over," the cryptic teachings in 1 Timothy 2:11–15 may at last make sense. The Greek word *authentein* appears only here, nowhere else in the entire New Testament. The term was used in secular Greek writings from before New Testament times, and it was used in a letter from the church father Clement of Alexandria. Its widespread secular use referred exclusively to the solicitation a prostitute makes in seducing a customer off the street. Far from meaning simply "teaching or having authority over," the language suggests using the worship setting for purposes of sexual seduction. We certainly would hope that Paul would object to such a practice. Since the Christian church is such a loving community, it is still appropriate to caution Christian women to love their brothers in the faith "pure and chaste from afar."

This risk of sexual seduction within the worshiping community was also what Clement of Alexandria was writing about when he used this word. He deplored the fact that Holy Communion and the love feast had, in some places, degenerated into a sex orgy.

Two churches, at Pergamos and Thyatira, were denounced because exactly the same encroachment of sexual seduction had contaminated them (Rev. 2:14, 20). Peter's cryptic allusion to "accursed children" in the context of the indictment of those "having eyes full of adultery" (2 Pet. 2:14), may provide further insight into this *authentein* passage in 1 Timothy. If these were converted but sexually addicted former prostitutes with their brood of fatherless children, the whole text becomes illuminated.

Consider too the strange conjunction of the sacred and profane in the teaching: "This is the will of God, your sanctification: that you should abstain from sexual immorality" (1 Thess. 4:3). This microcosm of biblical teaching on personal holiness contrasted as it is to the exploitation of other

---

[6]Gilbert Bilezikian, in *Beyond Sex Roles: A Guide for the Study of Female Roles in the Bible* (Grand Rapids: Baker, 1985), pp. 173-84. When we began to read through D. Bilezikian's book, it was almost too much to take in. We grabbed our Bibles to check out his interpretation, and ended up reading his extensive footnotes right along with the basic text.

people and the self, seems to say: Either you are "hungering and thirsting after righteousness/sanctification/holiness," or you are looking for endless self-gratification, with all of the waste of people along the way. St. Paul often uses such polarity words to summarize enormous truth.

Should the linguistic analysis and historical-rhetorical study bear out this interpretation[7] of the unique word *authentein*, then the passage in 1 Timothy would appear to be toward a special, self-sorted, identifiable segment of the church: converted and recovering sexual addicts. It could then be interpreted to say, "I do not permit a woman to evangelize using sexual seduction; such must be silent....But such women will be saved through faithfully rearing the children they have as they continue in faith, love, and holiness, with propriety."

Paul may have taken off the apostolic gloves to address a painful but persistent sexual problem in the early church, and one that continues to plague us. The connections between our sexuality and our spirituality are so complicated that patterns of past sexual behavior tend to persist and to invade the congregational domain unless explicit teaching names the risk and forbids the exploitation. I recall with pain the courageous meeting our pastor convened. A half dozen young married couples met to hear the pastor expose a sexual seduction that had been perpetrated by an institutional chaplain against one of our young ministers in training. All of those in the meeting had been supervised by the same chaplain. As the traumatized young man described the sexual seduction, it was clear that similar seductive steps had targeted without success each of the others. It is not easy to bring an ordained chaplain to repentance or rehabilitation, but it was essential to name the risk and bless those who had been targets of this man's *authentein*.

So Paul's principle in this passage is a valid one and needs to cut both ways. Both men and women are vulnerable to using ministry as a means of sexual seduction.

Silence, But Who?

We move to another Pauline passage that seems to advocate silencing women. First Corinthians 14:33–40 seems to be straightforward:

---

[7]For further discussion of *authentein* see Richard and Catherine Kroeger, "Ancient Heresies and a Strange Greek Verb," *Reformed Journal*, March 1979, pp. 12–14, and their "May Women Teach?" *Reformed Journal*, October 1980, p. 17.

[33]As in all the churches of the saints, the women should keep silence in the churches. For they are not permitted to speak, but should be subordinate, as even the law says. [34]If there is anything they desire to know, let them ask their husbands at home. For it is shameful for a woman to speak in the church. [35]What? Did the word of God originate with you, or are you the only ones it has reached?

[37]If any one thinks that he is a prophet, or spiritual, he should acknowledge that what I am writing to you is a command of the Lord. [38]If any one does not recognize this, he is not recognized. [39]So, my brethren, earnestly desire to prophesy, and do not forbid speaking in tongues; but all things should be done decently and in order. (RSV)

It seems odd that St. Paul would write these words since he has just outlined in 1 Corinthians 12 the specific ways a woman should wear her hair if she is going to speak or pray in public worship. At a first glance, this teaching seems clearly to violate his basic teaching that there is neither Jew nor Greek, male nor female in the kingdom of God. Paul everywhere else affirms women. He praises Dorcas, Lydia, and Priscilla for their part in spreading the gospel.

Is Paul schizophrenic? Why else would he praise women evangelists in one breath and then, forever silence women at worship and in the church? How can he do such a thing?

Because this passage is so contradictory of Paul's teaching and behavior many scholars regard it as likely not the work of Paul. Others attribute it to a cultural hangover from Jewish standards for men and women at worship.

But now a handful of scholars, independent of each other, have identified a repeated rhetorical pattern that runs through all of the first epistle to the Corinthians: Paul quotes his enemies, then attacks them, and then uses the language of sarcasm to refute them. He appears to be using a caustic literary strategy throughout this letter,[8] and the language of this passage fits that pattern.

Before looking at the caustic and combative structure of the passage, note what Robbie and I had missed for so long. Elsewhere Paul addresses

---

[8]See Bilezikian, *Beyond Sex Roles*, pp. 144–156, especially the correlating footnotes and citations he makes to other interpreters and interpretations of this text in 1 Corinthians 14:31–40.

believers as those "called to be saints" (Rom. 1:7). But here, "churches of the so-called saints" seems to be the derisive tone, as he attacks Judaizers who are following him around the Roman Empire, trying to turn new congregations of fledgling Christians into Jewish synagogues. Those Judaizers are harassing the young believers, wanting to force the men to be circumcised and to silence the women. "As even the law says" is a Judaistic appeal, not a Christian one. Nowhere else does Paul cite the "law" as the ultimate authority. Jesus, grace, love, forgiveness, and mutual submission are cardinal values with St. Paul. The role of women in 1 Corinthians 14 is identical to that of the role of women in the Jewish synagogue: absolute silence. They are told to ask for instruction at home.

The rhetorical structure of this passage is also striking and convincing. A single-letter Greek word is sprinkled through this passage. Looking much like our letter *n*, it is an *eta* and looks like this: η. Greek students today, unfortunately, are taught to translate it simply as "or." Thayer's Greek-English Lexicon opens with a description of its unique service:

> η, a disjunctive conjunction. Used to distinguish things or thoughts which either mutually exclude each other, or one of which can take the place of the other...before a sentence contrary to the one just preceding, to indicate that if one be denied or refuted the other must stand . . . .

"Or" is sometimes a disjunctive conjunction, for example: "Finish the job, or we will work overtime until it is done." More often, "or" is a mere connective. The tragedy of the translations after the KJV and RSV is that they all have gone to mere connective uses of "or." This blurs the passage and seems to make the Judaizers' teaching the "same as" Paul's caustic correction.

Before we show you the η locations in the 1 Corinthians 14 passage, we want you to reread the passage, as we did with Dr. Gilbert Bilezikian's help.[9] Remember this: Paul is writing 1 Corinthians in response to a report from Chloe's household (1:11) that serious divisions are splitting the young church. If you look for the η in the Greek text, you will see the list of heresies that angered Paul. In most of the cases noted here, Paul will first quote the heresy (without the helpful quotation marks we expect to find in today's

---

[9]Referring to Bilezikian's *Beyond Sex Roles*, pp. 144–156, work through these η passages in 1 Corinthians, pp. 144–56.

writing), as if to mock it as "truth." Then Paul attacks the heresy correcting it with his teaching, which follows each heresy. We will lift out a few of the Corinthian heresies, each followed by an η:

"I belong to Paul," "I belong to Apollos," "I belong to Cephas," "I belong to Christ" (1:12–14, 3:4, RSV).

"Every other sin which a man commits is outside the body; but the immoral man sins against his own body" (6:18, RSV).

"Food will not commend us to God. We are no worse off if we do not eat, and no better off if we do" (8:8, RSV).

The η shows up in the Greek text as a single-word sentence. Dr. Gilbert Bilezikian suggests that we read it as "Bunk!" The KJV and RSV catch most of these η disjunctions. The KJV translates them as, "What!" The RSV translates them as, "What?" If you read them as "bunk" or "nonsense," you get the disjunctive conjunction sense. Now here are the more complete texts with the η included:

> ¹If any of you has a dispute with another, dare he take it before the ungodly for judgment instead of before the saints? η. [Nonsense!] ²Do you not know that the saints will judge the world? ... ⁶But instead, one brother goes to law against another— and this in front of unbelievers!...η. [Nonsense!] ⁹Do you not know that the wicked will not inherit the kingdom of God? (6:1–2, 6, 9, NIV).

> ¹⁵Do you not know that your bodies are members of Christ himself? Shall I then take the members of Christ and unite them with a prostitute? η. [Never!] ¹⁶Do you not know that he who unites himself with a prostitute is one with her in body? For it is said, "The two will become one flesh." ¹⁷But he who unites himself with the Lord is one with him in spirit. (6:15–17, NIV)

> ¹⁸All other sins a man commits are outside his body, but he who sins sexually [is a fornicator] sins against his own body. η. [Nonsense!] ¹⁹Do you not know that your body is a temple of the Holy Spirit, who is in you, whom you have received from God? You are not your own; ²⁰you were bought at a price. Therefore honor God with your body. (6:18–20, NIV)

Finally, look at the passage in focus:

> [33]As in all the churches of the saints, [34]the women should keep silence in the churches. For they are not permitted to speak, but should be subordinate, as even the law says. [35]If there is anything they desire to know, let them ask their husbands at home. For it is shameful for a woman to speak in the church. [36]η. [What?] Did the word of God originate with you, or are you the only ones it has reached?

> [37]If any one thinks that he is a prophet, or spiritual, he should acknowledge that what I am writing to you is a command of the Lord. [38]If any one does not recognize this, he is not recognized. [39]So, my brethren, earnestly desire to prophesy, and do not forbid speaking in tongues; [40]but all things should be done decently and in order. (1 Cor. 14:33–40, RSV)

Paul appears to be using the double-trap argument here. He states the popular heresy, then mocks it (as if to say with η, a sarcastic "Nonsense!"). Then he follows with the correction to the bad teaching. Here and in 1 Corinthians 11, Paul becomes quite animated, and denounces anyone who dares to perpetuate the Judaizing nonsense he seeks to correct: "He is not recognized!"

Husbands as Chief Executive Officers of the Home?

We began our search for the meaning of "head" in Chapter 4, "'Head of the House': God's Order for Families?" We will look in depth at "head" as it describes the husband's relationship to the wife in Chapter 10, "'Head': Another Name for Husbands?" Here it will be enough simply to ask what image Paul and Peter may have had in mind when they used the term. A profound debate is presently underway among biblical scholars on the subject of the use of "head" by Paul.

In recent years, Stephen Bedale has been quoted widely as asserting that "head" nowhere is used metaphorically to denote "authority over," but to denote "source" or headwaters from which the stream originates.[10] Wayne

---

[10]Stephen Bedale, "The Meaning of Kephale in the Pauline Epistles," *Journal of Theological Studies*, no. 5, 1954, pp. 211–213.

Grudem marshaled a computer-based word search to analyze 2,336 examples of "head" in Greek literature, including the New Testament. He asserts that the New Testament Greek word for "head" (*kephale*) nowhere may be translated "source." Grudem says that in 16.2 percent of the "metaphoric uses" of the word, it actually refers to "person of superior authority or rank," or "ruler," "ruling part."[11]

After the first edition of this book appeared, we received an extensive letter from Richard Cervin, then teaching linguistics at the University of Illinois. His wife had bought our book and he read it with interest. He had recently completed a critique of Wayne Grudem's word search, but Cervin found that none of them supported the ideas of dominance or ruling over another person. Cervin's letter asked, "What agenda might a scholar have that would cause him to falsify his report?" His critique was submitted to the same journal in which Grudem's article had appeared, and we were furnished a pre-publication copy.[12]

My colleague for many years, Professor Fred Layman, also examined the 1 Corinthians 11 and Ephesians 5 passages and concluded that "headship" and "lordship" are not synonymous. Professor Layman says that those who confuse the two terms are overlooking Ephesians 5, where Paul teaches that the woman's submission to the husband is "as unto the Lord," not to the husband in any literal sense. Dr. Layman further notes that the entire Ephesians passage is focused on the radical change that Christianity required in male behavior: mutual submission, reverence, and care for their wives "as for their own bodies."[13]

Everyone agrees that Paul's "head" language is metaphoric. That is, Paul uses "head" to create an ordinary image to which we may liken a complicated, intangible reality. What is striking to us is that neither "source" nor "authority" is an immediate image that we would expect to be evoked with the metaphor of "head." And where the word *soma* (body) appears in

---

[11]Wayne Grudem, "Does Kephale Mean 'Source' or 'Authority Over' in Greek Literature: A Survey of 2,336 Examples," *Trinity Journal* 6, no. 1 (Spring 1985) 38–59. Grudem has also founded an organization devoted to protecting roles by which men rule over women.

[12]See Richard S. Cervin, "Does Kephale ('Head') Mean 'Source' or 'Authority Over' in Greek Literature? A Rebuttal," *Trinity Journal* 10:1, 1989, 19 pages.

[13]Fred Layman, "Male Headship in Paul's Thought," *Wesley Theological Society Journal* 15, no. 1 (Spring 1980): 46–67.

the same texts, the metaphor of the "head" cries out for the completing image of a "whole person"—i.e., the mystery of "two become one."

Herman Ridderbos agrees that there is implicit evidence suggesting the physiological metaphor; he regards it as untenable.[14] It is regrettable that Ridderbos rejects the simple connected metaphors of *kephale* and *soma*. And it is incredible that Grudem provided no category in his word search for simple anatomical, physiological uses of the word kephale. But we insist that the Genesis concept of "two become one" provides a striking and simple solution to the Corinthian and Ephesians texts. The Ephesians mystery of a head and a body that become one is powerfully portrayed in Revelation 21, as the bride dressed in fine linen comes "down out of heaven from God, prepared as a bride adorned for her husband" (v. 2). It is clear that the bride, the Last Woman, is the church, and equally clear that her Husband is the Last Man, Christ, the Lord of the church. This final mystery of "two become one" balances out the opening love story when the First Man and the First Woman became one. So the mystery of how a *kephale* and a *soma* form one whole and glorious person is the centerpiece of both human history and salvation history.

In this chapter we have laid out the New Testament texts that have been used to abuse both men and women, when those texts are isolated from the total teaching of Scripture. We have examined serious flaws and distortions of the interpretations, even in widely-accepted translations of the ancient texts. But we have looked at the total body of Scripture to establish the glorious, "two-become-one" image of Man and Woman in the "image of God," which is everywhere confirmed.

We commend to you the principle that says: If there seem to be contradictions between passages of Scripture, we know that the problem is ours—a human problem of perception. Robbie and I confess that we may not have considered the best data, or we may be biased in the ways we look at a text. Some of us live long enough to acquire experiential wisdom, which we try to apply to all times and circumstances, even when our experience contradicts Scripture. Given those fragile and tentative realities, we are surely obligated to take seriously the Creation and the Redemption images in Jesus. We ourselves are seriously impaired by living in a fallen world and living with psychological blinders that tend to make us ignore our own biases. So we dare not pontificate finally for you from the base of our own experience or reason alone.

---

[14]Herman Ridderbos, *Paul: An Outline of His Theology* (Grand Rapids: William B. Eerdmans, 1975), 380 ff.

Questions People Ask

Q: Isn't it odd that Jesus never really challenged the "traditional" role of the invisible woman in the synagogue—which then and now seems to have been entirely and exclusively a male enclave?

A: Perhaps Jesus did. You likely are familiar with the episode reported in Luke 10, and the altercation between Martha and Jesus about getting Mary into the kitchen where she belonged. Look at it.

> [38]Now as they went on their way, he entered a certain village, where a woman named Martha welcomed him into her home. [39]She had a sister named Mary, who sat at the Lord's feet and listened to what he was saying. [40]But Martha was distracted by her many tasks; so she came to him and asked, "Lord, do you not care that my sister has left me to do all the work by myself? Tell her then to help me." [41]But the Lord answered her, "Martha, Martha, you are worried and distracted by many things; [42]there is need of only one thing. Mary has chosen the better part, which will not be taken away from her." (Luke 10:38-42, NRSV)

Paint a picture of Mary in your mind. She is sitting "at the Lord's feet." This is the standard posture of a learner in the presence of a rabbi. One popular interpretation said, "Let thy house be a meeting house of the sages and sit amid the dust at their feet. Drink in their words, but talk not much at all with women." Here is the shocking fact: No rabbi would teach a woman, not even his own daughter. The movie *Yentl* moves on a plot in which a rabbi's daughter learns from the kitchen as her father teaches young men in the house. So moved by study of Hebrew language and scripture "from a distance," she succeeds in entering rabbinical school disguised as a man. Of this Luke passage, one commentator has said of Martha's complaint, "Mary was acting like a man!"

Yet for centuries preachers have contrasted the "spiritual" with the "temporal" in Mary and Martha while ignoring what Jesus called Mary's choosing "the better part." Dr. Eugene L. Lowry[15] reports that in Jesus' day,

---

[15]Dr. Eugene L. Lowry, "What Better Part?"(sermon delivered February 13, 2001 at Asbury Theological Seminary), available on videotape from Asbury Theological Seminary, 204 N. Lexington Avenue, Wilmore KY 40390. Phone (859) 858-3817 and request videotape No. 00B01V for 2/13/01. We have quoted the rabbinic and other views on women and study of Scripture directly from Dr. Lowry's sermon.

and in his culture, no woman was permitted to sit at the feet of a rabbi. In his amazing sermon, "What Better Part?" Lowry cited these several statements revealing the degrading of women in Jesus day. Two others he identified were rabbinic sayings: "Better to bury the Torah than to entrust it with a woman." "Better to teach your daughter lasciviousness, than to teach her the law." Lowry asserted that no commentator before 1970 paid any attention to the posture of Mary or the clear affirmation of her hunger for being taught by a rabbi. The social taboo of Jesus' day continued to cast a shadow over biblical interpretation until recent awakenings.

We can grieve over the evidence that Jesus' bold assertion that Mary's eligibility to study Scripture constituted "the better part," was entirely ignored in his culture in his time. But the larger grief is that for 2,000 years since then, commentators and teachers have failed to acknowledge the central message. Jesus was clearly empowering women for study and for ministry—the sole vocation for which study with a rabbi was preparation.

8

Head and Body:
The Complete Adam

We made a tour of Washington, D.C., our nation's capital, when our two sons were in first and fifth grades. After four days of saturation with the Smithsonian, the public national memorials and buildings, and the National Gallery of Art, we were all tired of looking. John and Mike were ready to do a sprint through the National Gallery, but Robbie and I were almost hypnotized in one room. It housed a single painting, Salvador Dali's *The Sacrament of the Last Supper*. The painting was not new to us, but its impressive size demanded attention that we had not given it before. We read the program guide on the painting and were dissatisfied, because the guide told us little about the symbolism of this great work of art.

In the painting, Jesus, blond and transparent at the thorax, is seated at the center of a table facing us. One hand gestures toward himself, and the other toward the ceiling. A glass of wine stands on the table in front of Jesus. A broken loaf of bread sits on the near edge of the table, the two halves a couple of feet apart. The heads of the twelve apostles are all bowed, showing no facial features. Only the crowns of their heads can be seen. Behind the figure of Jesus is what appears to be an open window with a strange dodecahedron, a twelve-sided opening that the Greek Pythagoreans declared to be the symbol of the universe. Through that open window we can see the edge of an ocean or a bay, in which islands of gigantic rock formations rise in a semicircle, arching toward us as if to encircle us. The painting is executed with dominant colors of white and blue. We notice through the transparent torso of Jesus that a fishing boat is tethered to the shore. The boat is at about the point where the heart of Jesus would be, if the transparent window through His body showed His interior body organs.

We notice suddenly that the heads of the apostles form an "arc" that, if extended and closed, would include us as we view the painting. The artist seems to imply that believers form the tightest, most intimate, perhaps most protected of all relationships with Jesus. We then notice that the rocky islands form yet another arc that, if extended to close another circle, would take in a gigantic area—perhaps the world, the tangible physical planet for which Jesus died.

Suspended in air above the entire scene at the supper table is a headless torso—another body. The top edge of the picture frame seems to have decapitated this body that is superimposed above everything, hanging between two worlds. Exactly. Here is the artist's image of the body of Christ, the church. The body remains "in the world," while the Head has taken temporary leave. The church is the visible body while the Head, Jesus Christ, is now invisible to our senses of sight and sound. We do not presently see Him, but the day will come when every eye "shall see His face" (Rev. 22:4).

In Dali's painting, the arms of the body are distended to encompass the table, Jesus, and apostles. So we are drawn into the sacramental feast simply by viewing it in the room. Salvador Dali has made his point: The body of Jesus continuing in the world is Christ's bride, the church. And we may be sure the body remains attached to the Head, which is temporarily "out of the picture" and invisible to us.[1] In Chapter 2, we painted again the Creation images of the splitting of the original Adam. In the book, *Bonding: Relationships in the Image of God*, we referred to the "First Adam" as if he were the left end of a pair of bookends enclosing Holy Scripture. At the other stands Jesus, the "Last Adam."

Since Genesis 2 uses human anatomy—head and body—as a metaphor to explain the complex relationships between Man and Woman, we will

---

[1] "The Sacrament of the Last Supper" was created by Salvador Dali at the suggestion of Chester Dale, who suggested it in 1954 when Dale was president of the National Gallery of Art. For those who would wish to probe the philosophical roots of the painting, it would be appropriate to consult Salvador Dali's autobiography, *The Secret Life of Salvador Dali* (New York: Dial Press, 1942). There he writes that by 1941, he was forsaking surrealism as bankrupt, along with the collectivist, atheist, and neopagan utopias, which he had studied in the writings of Karl Marx and Rosenberg, the Nazi. After studying theology, Dali began to believe that the spiritual forces for the reconstruction of Europe lay in "a reactualization of the Catholic, European, Mediterranean tradition." The painting, when we studied it in the mid-sixties, was hanging in Gallery 60-B, the Chester Dale Collection, of the National Gallery of Art, Washington, D.C., USA.

likely miss the mark if we ignore the detail of the images there. Physiology is a witness of the Creation. So we should not mistrust the apparent biology of the metaphor, dismissing the Creation text as being so metaphoric as to have little connection with the real world.

Eden is God's "operating room." The Adam contains the only human "stuff" created by God. No new material is introduced. There is no second dip into "dust," no grafting from another linkage in the life chain outlined in the first chapter of Genesis.

Here the images are impressive: The original Adam is stretched out for the surgery. God is the Surgeon. The Adam is the patient. The Lord God presides over the anesthesia. The Adam's thorax (the *pleura*) is opened. The Divine Surgeon builds up the woman from the cellular material removed from the Adam. The woman thus contains the same genetic material as the original Adam. God presents the woman as a mirror image of the man. Man is evoked to the first recorded human speech: "Bone of my bones and flesh of my flesh; she shall be called Woman" (Gen. 2:23).

Woman is God's transformational clone of Man. Notice that Man's pronouncement in biological terms ("bone of bones, flesh of flesh") marks her as twinlike with himself. Creative geniuses who write science fiction have not come close to matching this mystery.

Adam as Head and Body

We cannot miss the almost shadowlike central focus that goes immediately to Man and to Woman. Man is a speaking being, who visually concentrates on Woman. Woman is distinctly formed from cellular material from the thorax of the Adam—from the "kinder and gentler part." It is easy (though potentially dangerous) to note some innate differences in these polar opposites:

1. Males tend to score high as "thinkers" and females as "feelers" when standardized tests of those polarities are used.[2] Both use cognitive processes equally, but in significantly different ways. Women, taken as a group, are more likely to filter their reasoning through a concern for people and to

---

[2]Continuing study of sex differences tends to pare away many cultural and learned differences. But the bottom line now includes not only the genital differentiation, but its compounding effects in bone development affecting height, muscle versus fatty tissue development affecting body build, and also brain development and utilization. Somewhere within this morass of complicated but subtle differences lies "affect" or feelings. Women tend more consistently to depend on

weigh their decisions in view of what happens to the people as a result of those decisions.

2. Males tend to take an "objective" lookout-tower approach to life. They readily give advice, while females are more likely to take an empathetic, "subjective" perspective and listen. Women tend to complain that their husbands cannot simply listen to them when they have had a bad day. The man feels obligated to "fix it" by giving advice, or even by taking immediate and direct action himself.[3]

3. Males tend to look out for, protect, and deal with potential threats to their families by intercepting the invaders at a distance. In contrast, females are more likely to hover over their loved ones, ready to "defend to the death." They most often engage intruders inside the nest. When the crisis is past, women tend to turn to nurturing and encompassing the threatened object of their protection even when there is no presenting problem on which to focus the caregiving. The child or husband who has thus been saved often walks away grateful, but unable to receive the abundant, affectionate care that the woman offers.

What we see when we look at this male-female division of gifts and services is at least analogical to the metaphor of "splitting the Adam." In Hebrew thought throughout the Old Testament, for example, the seat of emotions was believed to reside in the bowels. Kidneys were given a special role, believed to have a higher function—similar to our use of "heart" as the seat of emotions today. The "heart" in Hebrew thought was considered the center of moral reasoning and choice, not emotion. It would be easy to conclude that the Westernizing of our understanding has conferred all of these functions to the brain. This shrinks our conception of ourselves. We think of a human being as a sort of top-heavy robot, whose only significant operations occur inside the "head."

"people concerns" when making judgments than do men, who tend to depend more on rational, even mathematical issues. This occurs at a 60 to 40 percent split for both when comparing "feeling" to "thinking" in the research that lies beneath the Myers-Briggs Personality Profile. To examine the statistical data see David Kiersey and Marilyn Bates in *Please Understand Me: Character and Temperament Type* (Prometheus Nemesis, Box 2082, Del Mar, Calif. 92014).

[3] See Ken Druck, *Secrets Men Keep* (Garden City, N.Y.: Doubleday, 1985). In a *Chicago Tribune* interview, Dr. Druck reported that he finds most men helplessly locked in a "fix-it" mode. They have difficulty listening with empathy to anyone, but tend to feel it is their obligation to rescue the speaker from his or her trouble, often with an outpouring of verbal advice.

But in Eden, when the two became "one flesh, naked and unashamed," we see an image of wholeness—specifically, of a primeval holiness and mutuality by which the unique, newly differentiated powers also formed "one whole person." "Headship" and "bodyship" in Eden were clearly created to look like something more unified than General Motors Corporation and the United Auto Workers union.

Two Become One: The Mystery of Complementarity

In Eden, the miracle of "two become one" denoted forever the ideal of full complementarity. There was no suggestion that either individual ought to become like the other. But God demonstrated that their differences could fill in their individual deficits, yielding the stunning portrayal of a full and completed humanity.

These differentiated partners were reunited specifically at the unique point of their differentiation: their sexuality. Identity in each of us is so deeply connected with our sexuality that the giving and uniting with another person at the genital level denote the ultimate, final surrender of the self to the other. We should not be surprised to learn that human blood types are visible in analysis of reproductive material. Nor should it be surprising that deadly diseases can move through intimate body fluids into the bloodstream of a sexual partner.

By the gesture of one-flesh intimacy, lovers are granted the franchise to participate in the mystery of Creation. Their child forever denotes the eternal dimensions of their union. But the gestures of loving that united two persons sexually leave the intangible bond by which they know, as if instinctually, that they have "become one flesh." The bonding is present in young lovers or old. Only the sexual addict, the promiscuous person, is insensitive to the significance of such bonding. Persons have become objects.[4]

When the bonding attraction of "opposites" is healthy and the two lovers are nicely settled in ego development and wholeness, you will see each tending to what he or she does best. As if by reflex, the male is inclined to be the protector and problem solver. The female is similarly inclined to look after her own and her husband's more interior needs, which are often invisible to people who do not know him well. St. Paul notes these

---

[4]That story and a path for recovery and renewal are set out in my book, *Re-Bonding: Preventing and Restoring Damaged Relationships.*

differences in his famous description of how each submits to the other in Ephesians 5. He says the wife submits to the husband as "head," just as the church honors Jesus as its "Head." But the husband lays down his life to protect the wife, loving her "as he loves his own body." The anatomical metaphor is complete. Body and head form one whole person. They are one. While their instinctual, Creation-gifted motivations to serve each other differ toward their unique polarities, they are mutually interdependent, as is the head-and-body unit in which each of us lives and moves.

So watch for the wonder when the mystery of sexual bonding is underway. You will see it on the faces of both younger and older lovers, and you will know that it denotes the attraction of opposites who together form the mystery of "two become one flesh."

Servanthood as Submission and Synchronicity: The Dance of Marriage

Here we confront a basic principle that undergirds the Creation gift of our mutually dependent sexuality and that must also form the foundation for our continuing relationship in marriage. The marital principle also forms a microcosm from which we can infer all other human relationships, and the family system is the primary rehearsal and formation arena for our participation in larger social systems.

The principle is this: *Whole persons form mutually interdependent relationships with those whose gifts differ from their own.* They enter into those relationships noncompetitively but reverently. They participate in the relationships spontaneously, almost naively, assuming that they enjoy the same equitable acceptance and respect that they extend to the other. Whole persons both listen and initiate conversation. They can debate without name-calling or put-downs. And when the best has been offered all around, they can consolidate, contribute to decisions, and eagerly implement what the consensus has produced, owning it without clinging to an individualistic, peevish personal perspective they refuse to modify.

In this chapter we have looked at the "head" and "body" metaphors straight out of anatomy. We cannot escape seeing the futility of adversary struggles over power. We see, every morning in the mirror, the image that Scripture has held up to us: the absolute necessity for each part of the physical person to be cared for, so as to assure that it serves all others parts well. "Love your spouse as you love your own body," is a call to understand—and a summons to celebrate—the unity, the collegiality, and the synchrony of marriage. Any preoccupation with any other symbolism of "head" should quickly wither in light of the central pictures of human life from Eden until now.

Questions People Ask

Q. *You make me a little nervous with all of this "biology" mixed with theology. Are you buying into "biological determinism?"*

A. Biological determinism holds that anatomy and biology control all of life. That is precisely what we reject. We reject too the idea that anyone can get theology simply by rational deduction and ignore the biological evidences of God's Creation. For this reason, we speak often of the three witnesses that must ultimately come into agreement: Creation, Scripture, and Jesus. We reject determinism of all kinds, including what might claim to be rooted in any one of the three witnesses while ignoring the others—all three come from God. We are always eager to examine the troublesome questions and the puzzle of life, and we call on the witnesses to speak. We are especially eager to identify the harmonious way that biology, theology, and faith may unite to enrich us all.

9

Jesus Has a Plan for Families

Sitting there in the gigantic men's Bible study at Lovers Lane United Methodist Church in Dallas, I was in theological shock. I'm afraid I took the "introvert's jet plane" and left the innocent and gentle Exxon executive who was expounding "God's Order for Families" from the book of Esther. I had my Bible in my lap. Suddenly, I was seeing minor points in the story that I had missed in my marathon readings of the Old Testament. The story took on fresh dimensions to me.[1] The businessman was treating the tragic, heathen words from the book of Esther as "foundational" for the godly home, but it had never occurred to me to read the words of a pagan king as stating the will of God. Look at the passage again.

> [1]The events here related happened in the days of Ahasuerus, the Ahasuerus who ruled from India to Ethiopia, a hundred and twenty-seven provinces. [2]At this time he sat on his royal throne in Susa the capital city. [3]In the third year of his reign he gave a banquet for all his officers and his courtiers; and when his army of Persians and Medes, with his nobles and provincial governors, were in attendance, [4]he displayed the wealth of his kingdom and the pomp and splendour of his majesty for many days, a hundred and eighty in all.

---

[1]We opened this story and quoted the text from the book of Esther at the beginning of Chapter 4.

⁵When those days were over, the king gave a banquet for all the people present in Susa, the capital city, both high and low; it was held in the garden court of the royal pavilion and lasted seven days. ⁶There were white curtains and violet hangings fastened to silver rings with bands of fine linen and purple; there were alabaster pillars and couches of gold and silver set on a mosaic pavement of malachite and alabaster, of mother-of-pearl and turquoise. ⁷Wine was served in golden cups of various patterns: the king's wine flowed freely as befitted a king, ⁸and the law of the drinking was that there should be no compulsion, for the king had laid it down that all the stewards of his palace should respect each man's wishes. ⁹In addition, Queen Vashti gave a banquet for the women in the royal apartments of King Ahasuerus.

¹⁰On the seventh day, when he was merry with wine, the king ordered Mehuman, Biztha, Harbona, Bigtha, Abagtha, Zethar, and Carcas, the seven eunuchs who were in attendance on the king's person, ¹¹to bring Queen Vashti before him wearing her royal crown, in order to display her beauty to the people and the officers; for she was indeed a beautiful woman. ¹²But Queen Vashti refused to come in answer to the royal command conveyed by the eunuchs. This greatly incensed the king, and he grew hot with anger.

¹³Then the king conferred with his wise men versed in misdemeanours; for it was his royal custom to consult all who were versed in law and religion, ¹⁴those closest to him being Carshena, Shethar, Admatha, Tarshish, Meres, Marsena, and Memucan, the seven princes of Persia and Media who had access to the king and held first place in the kingdom. ¹⁵He asked them, "What does the law require to be done with Queen Vashti for disobeying the command of King Ahasuerus brought to her by the eunuchs?" ¹⁶Then Memucan made answer before the king and the princes: "Queen Vashti has done wrong, and not to the king alone, but also to all the officers and to all the peoples in all the provinces of King Ahasuerus. ¹⁷Every woman will come to know what the queen

has done, and this will make them treat their husbands with contempt; they will say, 'King Ahasuerus ordered Queen Vashti to be brought before him and she did not come.' [18]The great ladies of Persia and Media, who have heard of the queen's conduct, will tell all the king's officers about this day, and there will be endless disrespect and insolence! [19]If it pleases your majesty, let a royal decree go out from you and let it be inscribed in the laws of the Persians and Medes, never to be revoked, that Vashti shall not again appear before King Ahasuerus; and let the king give her place as queen to another who is more worthy than she. [20]Thus when this royal edict is heard through the length and breadth of the kingdom, all women will give honour to their husbands, high and low alike."

[21]Memucan's advice pleased the king and the princes, and the king did as he had proposed. [22]Letters were sent to all the royal princes, to every province in its own script and to every people in their own language, in order that each man might be master in his own house and control all his own womenfolk. (Esther 1:1–22, NEB)

What was the setting in which this "vertical marriage" decree came down from King Ahasuerus? It was so embarrassing that even our presenter, the Exxon executive, apologized for the "context." Look at the details:

1. The king had thrown an open house for six months—180 days. Political and military leaders from the entire empire were present.

2. The climax of the six-month party was an intensive week-long banquet. It included all guests from the least to the greatest.

3. The guests were saturated with liquors suited to the taste of each. Each guest had a private wine steward, or server, to guarantee that the drinking preferences were followed in detail.

4. Queen Vashti was hosting a parallel banquet for the women in the royal palace.

5. On the final day, king Ahasuerus was intoxicated with his drinking, and he commanded the seven personal attendants to bring in Queen Vashti for the pleasure of his guests—wearing her royal crown. "She was indeed a beautiful woman."

6. The queen refused for reasons that are not stated, but implied: the king was regarding her as an instrument, an object, and was arbitrarily interrupting her own event to boost his own status before his guests. Was he also wanting to tease his well-fed and drunken guests with her potential as a sex object?

7. The king was "greatly incensed" and "grew hot with anger."

8. Memucan seized the moment to cite legal charges against the queen: The queen had disobeyed the king, and this would be a negative role model for all of the women in the empire.

9. So the decree was written in the irrevocable laws of the Persians and the Medes, posted in every public place: "Each man might be master in his own house and control all his own womenfolk."

I could see why the Exxon lecturer apologized for the setting of this story, yet it did not deter him from claiming it as an authoritative teaching for marriage and family relationships. I wondered what the lecturer might have said if someone had asked whether it was right that Esther was about to marry this drunken bum of a newly divorced king. But then, I have never heard a sermon on Queen Esther that addresses the king's painful divorce and remarriage. I was being cynical. But my reflection suddenly exposed the key question that I knew I had to answer: Where can we find a distinctly Christian model of the family for today?

Does Jesus Have a Word?

I returned to the car pool with my hosts for the evening. Huddled in the rear seat, I was deep in thought. *Surely*, I thought, *there must be a clear teaching from Jesus that throws light on this kind of abuse of power, this arbitrary assumption that husbands can use their wives, employers can use employees, and one social class can exploit another. What is the word from Jesus?*

Before our car had completed the return trip from Lovers Lane in Dallas, I was sure my mental computer had located a passage I needed to consult. I shudder to think that without that night of insult to Christian teaching I might never have been cornered into reflecting on Jesus' solution. Look at these words of Jesus, responding to an appeal that two of His disciples be given places of authority in His coming kingdom:

> [20]Then the mother of the sons of Zebedee came to him with her sons, and kneeling before him, she asked a favor of him.

²¹And he said to her, "What do you want?" She said to him, "Declare that these two sons of mine will sit, one at your right hand and one at your left, in your kingdom." ²²But Jesus answered, "You do not know what you are asking. Are you able to drink the cup that I am about to drink?" They said to him, "We are able." ²³He said to them, "You will indeed drink my cup, but to sit at my right hand and at my left, this is not mine to grant, but it is for those for whom it has been prepared by my Father."

²⁴When the ten heard it, they were angry with the two brothers. ²⁵But Jesus called them to him and said, "You know that the rulers of the Gentiles lord it over them, and their great ones are tyrants over them. ²⁶It will not be so among you; but whoever wishes to be great among you must be your servant, ²⁷and whoever wishes to be first among you must be your slave; ²⁸just as the son of Man came not to be served but to serve, and to give his life a ransom for many." (Matt. 20:20–28, NRSV)

And a more shocking paraphrase is found in Kenneth Taylor's *Living Bible*: "Among the heathen, kings are tyrants and each minor official lords it over those beneath him. But among you it is quite different." In a single, sweeping teaching, Jesus disconnects the redeemed person from traditional, power-based ways of relating to others. He does it in a way that applies to every human relationship, including marriage and family.

These days it is quite common to hear Christian teachings on "servanthood." Regrettably, many apply it only to evangelism or to Christian social responsibility in the world outside the home. The idea of a "servant" marriage rarely seems to occur to us males who have been captivated by servanthood as a model for ministry. "Servant," it turns out, is usually translated from a Greek term literally meaning "slave." It is related to the word *submission*, which so many males want applied exclusively to females. The *Living Bible* calls such power domination the perspective of the "heathen." It is a secular power structure rather than a Christian servant structure.

At What Price the Vertical, Model for Marriage and Family?

Look at the context for Jesus' teaching about servant relationships, as an alternative to power-brokering our way to success:

1. The "mother of the sons of Zebedee" (a fallen, power-oriented social order that regarded the woman and the children as property of the husband) came to Jesus with her sons. Kneeling down (the posture of deference) she asked a favor of Jesus (full of apologies for bothering him).

2. "Declare that these two sons of mine will sit, one at your right hand and one at your left, in your kingdom," she begged.

3. Jesus responded with a question about whether they were able to drink of the cup He would have to drink, to suffer with Him. The young sons warmed up to the challenge, replying, "We are able." (A popular song, sung by a million Christian youth at evening worship, echoes the phrase. But it completely misses the arrogance and wrongheadedness of the sons of Zebedee.)

4. Jesus guaranteed them that they would have to "drink the cup" with Him, but then He had to disappoint them by admitting that He had no authority to make the power appointments they wanted. That was a task only his Father could accomplish.

5. The other ten disciples "were angry with the two brothers." That power-centered event evoked the succinct and radically Creation-based statement of a principle about human relationships and the use of power. Consider the high price of verticalizing any relationship, whether a marriage or a corporation:

The secular power model feeds pride. Watch the next "search committee" process at your favorite organization or educational institution. When the racehorses have been vetted and trotted around the viewing arena and the winner announced, there is a "winner." The others are "not winners," but have been set up in the horse-race situation that will forever separate them from the person who once may have been a true colleague.

We worked for many years with a Christian statesman who wanted all conversations to be informal and exploratory, until the person had been found who would be the only candidate for the position. At first we regarded the process as devious, especially when he prepared a group of us to host a guest at a series of meals on campus. But the president's final caution to us was a profound disclosure of protection for the dignity of the guest: "Our guest has a fine reputation. If we decide after these informal conversations with him that he comes up short on some small, but crucial qualification, it must never be said that he interviewed for the job and was rejected. You are the evaluation team, but he is not an official candidate. He is on campus as our guest. Do you have any questions?" We were stunned, but we had no questions. It was clear that persons are more important to this man than institutional pride.

The secular power model with its "win-lose" competition breeds hostility. The ten remaining disciples were provoked to jealousy by the thought that two of their number were principals in a power-grab play. Original sin lurks and triggers competition in our veins, sometimes to our surprise. We show it by the way we drive, by the way we negotiate stoplights, and by our addictions to competition as innocent as soccer or basketball. If you want to see the measure of original sin, just watch a group of male seminary graduate students play pickup basketball before their wives and other campus women. If bishops and other ecclesial positions are won competitively, you can easily predict the future of that denomination.

The secular power model exploits people. It is inevitable that the people "down the ladder" in the chain of command get used. Whether it is a marriage, an official church board, or a corporation, power brokers use the people "beneath them." There are reports to be written, menial tasks to be done, and the job description that mandates "any other tasks as delegated by the supervisor." In the truly heathen model, the assignments are arbitrary, urgently needed at once, without appropriate compensation, and ghostwirtten so as to credit the boss as if he had completed the task single-handedly.

The exploitation may be more subtle. Even our use of titles sometimes suggests who the second-class citizens are. One pastor illustrated this when he reported how his congregation had wrestled with pastoral titles as they added more ordained clergy to the staff. There was an extended debate over whether the second full-time staff member would be designated Associate Pastor or Assistant Pastor. Then someone broke the deadlock by reminding the deliberating group that it did not make much difference, since the abbreviation for both titles would be the same. Titles in themselves tended to denote either exaltation or exploitation. So the congregation determined to refer to all ministry staff by one title: Pastor. Their reasoning was compelling. The service given would earn the honor and status appropriate to the community's life; titles could never guarantee either. To attempt to discriminate among Christian leaders by pitting them against one another in a "horse race" or by using layered titles is to play out the heathen tendencies we all have. While it appears to build a sense of high self-respect among the winners, it produces another effect:

The secular power model wastes resources. Benevolent monarchs in the corporate world invite "suggestions" from the "subjects," often paying rewards for ideas for improving the profit position of the company. Sometimes the underling is made employee of the week or given a prime parking space for a week. Corporate executives may use these ostensible "perks" as a way to manipulate employees.

In a marriage, when either partner is coerced or compelled to submit, the result is a loss of perspective, resources, and imagination. Secular competitive management not only deploys the chief executive officer to an absurdly lonely position, sitting atop the totem pole, the lonely executive is also deprived of the richness of basic information and dialogue that might have made the ship unsinkable.

In vertical marriages where one partner is coercively dominated by the other, everybody loses. The oppressed spouse retreats to the world within, filled with emotions that range from rage to passive indifference with resulting atrophy and waste. The domineering spouse is perpetually in the position of having to make all decisions, take responsibility for any failures, possess all intelligence, and do all of it instantly.

In 1974, we were impressed by a unique feature in the marriage ceremony of Julie Cutler and our son John. They had forged a set of poetic lines and dropped them in the middle of a traditional service. The lines were adapted from Kahlil Gibran's classic, *The Prophet.*[2]

> I feel as if we were born together, and will
>   be together forever.
> We will be together when the white wings of death
>   shall scatter our days.
> and we will still be together in the arms of God.
>
> I will love you, but will not make a bondage of love.
> Let us make our love into a moving sea

[2]Adapted from Kahlil Gibran, "The Prophet" (New York: Alfred A. Knopf, 1963), 15–16.

between the shores of our souls.
Let us sing and dance together and be joyous,
    but let us each remain ourselves.
Even as the strings of a lute are alone
    though they quiver with the same music.
Let us stand together,
    yet not too near together.
Let us remember that the pillars of the temple
    stand apart,
And the oak tree and the cypress grow together,
    but not in each other's shadow.

The secular power model is explicitly condemned by Jesus. Perhaps that is enough. But Jesus was not one to be arbitrary. He knew much more than we have described here about how ineffective the heathen/power model is in marriages, families, churches, and corporations.

The late Professor Gilbert James, my colleague at Asbury Seminary for many years, once delivered a campus lecture whose main focus was the central tendency of all institutions toward the demonic—toward the abuses characteristic of the evil which St. Paul warned about in Ephesians 6:12. That evil is all around us: "our struggle is not against enemies of blood and flesh, but against the rulers, against the authorities, against the cosmic powers of this present darkness, against the spiritual forces of evil in the heavenly places" (NRSV).

A few months later, at a ministers' training event in the Detroit area Professor James documented the tendencies toward evil in all organizations. During the closing talk-back time, he shared the platform with a denominational executive who had explained the organizational chart of the whole church. That chart stood on a large easel nearby. As the moderator fielded questions from conference participants, one was directed to Dr. James: "What would you suggest for our denomination and its organizational structure, since you said that all institutions have a central tendency toward becoming demonic power machines?"

Without a word, Gilbert James rose from the table where he was seated with the episcopal guest. He moved to the organizational chart. Then, grasping it top and bottom, he flipped the chart upside down. When he was seated again, he said, "I think that would be a good place to start."

Exactly. Jesus said the same thing. Let us regard ordination as the "lowest order." The only lower position would be that of area supervisor or bishop. Just as a tree delivers its fruit on the network of complex branches where the light and sun mix, so also the tree draws its resources from below, where the servant roots do their hidden, supportive nurturing work.[3]

What Kind of Chain for Making Decisions?

Wherever people work in pairs or groups, some game plan has to be devised to distribute the responsibilities and to check on what happens to strategic jobs that must be done. Since the vertical chain of command is condemned by Jesus, then how are those responsibilities and accountabilities to be handled? Here are some structures and strategies we have worked through. For the marriage and family, a diagram of the Jesus model might look like this:

Consider these features of such a working relationship:

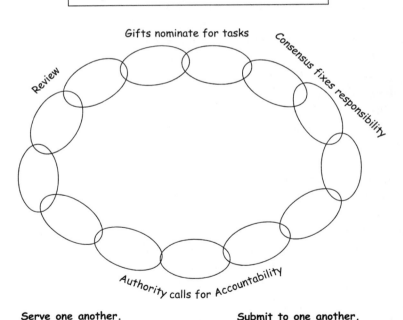

Fig. C - A Servant-Submission Chain

Gifts nominate for tasks

Consensus fixes responsibility

Review

Authority calls for Accountability

Serve one another.   **Submit to one another.**

[3]See Gilbert James, "The Use and Abuse of Power: A Study in Principalities and Powers," *The Asbury Seminarian* 30, no. 1 (October 1975): 6–23.

1. Gifts, not gender or seniority, nominate for responsibility.

2. Consensus, sometimes with trial periods for experimentation, fixes responsibility.

3. Authority goes with the assignment, and implies regular feedback and accountability.

4. Evaluation and review are by consensus and may lead to a redistribution of responsibility to better match gifts and energy, now based on experience and review. The structures will not work unless they are supported by:

5. Absolute mutual respect. Respect goes to persons, with additional respect given for services performed for the common good—not to the office or job titles.

6. Consistent mutual submission.

Who Makes Final Decisions?

In any organization or ongoing set of relationships, certain responsibilities "go with the territory." Where authority has been fixed by consensus (that is, by mutual respect agreement), it is clear that the responsibilities to make decisions belong to that person. In the most complex organizations, even a heathen one, a chief executive officer could not possibly make all of the decisions alone. It is inconceivable that any committee of two (e.g., a marriage) would elect officers. Some guidelines might look like this:

Who Makes the Decision?

1. The person to whom responsibility and authority has been assigned by prior consensus.

2. By marital consensus, if the decision is regarded as too complex or far-reaching for either spouse to act alone.

3. If there is no consensus, postpone until there is consensus. Make no decision until both spouses own it.

When people respect each other, they will not demand a quick decision or take things into their own hands to satisfy their appetite for instant gratification. Instead of serving as a sort of "veto power," when mutual respect and mutual submission are in place, reluctance is recognized by the other spouse as a legitimate reason to wait. A comment such as, "Until you feel really right about this, we won't go forward with it," becomes wisdom grounded in gracious patience. But if one spouse nags, taunts, or tries to hurry a reluctant spouse, the relationship suffers. Manipulation through use of shame or guilt, can dissolve the trust in a "two become one" mystery marriage. So mutual respect and mutual submission always mean: "If you cannot get the consent of your mind or heart right now, we need to wait, even let this opportunity pass." In a marriage, that attitude carries a deeper meaning: " You are more important to me than having what I want right now."

Mirror, Mirror on the Wall, Who Is the Powermonger?

It is the nature of egocentrism and of original sin that our deepest motivations sometimes remain hidden from us. One effort to study motivation for moral action is a research field called "moral development" or "moral reasoning" and "structuralism." This research shows that a healthy person makes moral choices on the basis that he or she would be willing to trade places with anyone affected by the decision. That is ultimate "fairness." This personal quality is called "perspectivism," the ability to see things from many points of view at the same time.

Most of us need mentors, confidential moral and spiritual advisors to whom we can say, "Let me tell you what I am feeling or what I am about to do. Ask me everything that comes to mind. I do not trust myself to be objective about this whole thing."

M. Scott Peck reveals the opposite side of this issue in his first-draft psychiatric definition of "evil" titled *People of the Lie*. It may be all the more compelling because Dr. Peck wrote this without a significant theological or biblical background, only recently having requested Christian baptism. Peck describes clinical evil this way:

a. Consistent destructive, scape-goating behavior, which may often be quite subtle.

b. Excessive, albeit usually covert, intolerance to criticism and other forms of narcissistic injury.

c. Pronounced concern with a public image and self-image of respectability, contributing to a stability of lifestyle but also to pretentiousness and denial of hateful feelings or vengeful motives.

d. Intellectual deviousness, with an increased likelihood of a mild schizophrenic-like disturbance of thinking at times of stress. [4]

Peck offers a caution to those of us who live and move within a self-avowed religious tradition. "We come now to a sort of paradox," Peck writes. "I have said that evil people feel themselves to be perfect. At the same time, however, I think they have an unacknowledged sense of their own evil nature. Indeed it is this very sense from which they are frantically trying to flee." [5] He suggests that we learn to detect the reality of evil by the smoothness of its disguise. Since the primary motive of evil is disguise, one of the most likely places to find evil people of high ambition is in the church. Where better to hide?

Perhaps the disciples' question at the Last Supper is not merely rhetorical. "Lord, is it I?" is always appropriate. "Show me my heart," the honest believer asks. "I am too embroiled in the whole tangle of life to know my own motivation."

In a direct validating contrast to Peck's psychiatric definition of evil are the conclusions of faith development researcher Professor James W. Fowler of Emory University. In describing adult Christian maturity, he asserts that such a "vocation" is a call "to personhood in relationships. There is no personal fulfillment that is not part of a communal fulfillment. We find ourselves by giving ourselves....Christians see our potential as humans to be represented, as it says in Ephesians 4:13, 'in a mature personhood that partakes of the measure of the stature which belongs to the fullness of Jesus Christ.'" Fowler identifies specific characteristics of Christian maturity in wonderful contrast to Peck's "evil" domain:

a. Devoted to excellence without competition.

b. Freedom—beyond jealousy—to rejoice in all excellence, the gifts and graces of others.

c. Freedom to do our work, pursue our destiny, finding myriad ways to join God's activity.

d. Freedom from having to please everybody.

---

[4] M. Scott Peck, *People of the Lie* (New York: Simon & Schuster, 1983), 129.

[5] Ibid., 76–77.

e. Called to seek and maintain a responsible balance in the investment of our time and energy.

f. Seeing time as a gift, therefore life and death are only markers, boundaries on the gift.

g. Seeing the human and Christian vocation, ever refining, ever changing its focus.[6]

In this chapter, we have explored Jesus' word on relationships and attempted to distinguish between Christian principles and pagan models. We have invited you to put popular teachings about the "chain of command" into the perspective of both Creation and gospel. We then asked you to explore Jesus' way of leading by both service and submission. We have more to learn about the biblical teachings, but we have a clear word from Matthew 20 governing all relationships and distinguishing between Jesus' model and the heathen model.

All of this leaves us with a dream of what every marriage might become. Several years ago brooding over some of these issues, we developed a statement of what we imagine is a universal marital dream:

> The marriage we long for is one in which
> together we can be sure
> of the best decisions,
> the fullest set of options,
> the most balanced perspective,
> the best resourced effort.
> Such a marriage means absolute
> trust,
> honesty,
> integrity,
> and mutual respect.
> It means that neither of us alone is
> always right,
> always strong,
> always the leader, or
> always the follower.
> But together we can face anything.

---

[6]James W. Fowler, *Becoming Adult, Becoming Christian: Adult Development and Christian Faith* (San Francisco: Harper & Row, 1984), 102–105.

Questions People Ask

Q. *I've always felt responsible for making decisions for my family. How can I go about helping my wife and children become responsible for part of our decisions?*

A. Bravo! Everyone in your family will thank you for bringing them "on line" in responsibility. Teachers and future employers of your children will praise you when they see good self-control, excellent work habits, and readiness to take responsibility for what happens, whether it turns out well or badly. At our house, we made lists of things that need to be done, then decided who had the skills and time to do the job entirely by themselves. If they volunteered, they got the nod to carry through. Children deserve to have daily and weekly "work lists" of their responsibilities. Really tough jobs need to be a team effort—a parent and a child together, for example, or both spouses teamed up to knock out some really huge challenge. A refrigerator-door list of chores is often enough to jog memory and get the energy online.

Q. *Isn't "final responsibility" too strong to use for a woman's or a child's carrying out assigned tasks?*

A. It would be if the husband and father were the "chief executive officer" of the family, as many people suggest he should be. If he were, it would be the husband's job to delegate the authority and responsibility; but if the person failed, then he would have to take responsibility for making a bad delegation or assignment, then do the work himself. This is common practice in managing a corporation, but is not effective even there. And it is deadly in the family. In the first place, the husband and father must carry the full load of all responsibilities if he adopts that CEO model. Worse, the wife and the children are forever dependent, prevented from becoming truly and fully human through participation in the life of the family and the household. Jesus' principle was to teach the disciples everything He knew. That should be every parent's goal with children. It is every spouse's goal with the beloved spouse. If the home is the "school" for preparation for making adult decisions, then absolute final authority must be given, with enough room for both good and poor decisions. Then the consequences can be brought right back to the person who had full responsibility for making those decisions. In days when most children grew up on the farm, caring for livestock—feeding and watering and housing—was a "final moral choice" that children learned early to manage.

Q. *I like your picture and explanation of the "circular chain" of family responsibilities, but how would it work exactly?*

A. First of all, this kind of dynamic in a family requires a lot of listening. It depends on asking questions instead of short-circuiting conversations. Mutual respect is going to take a little more time and a lot more courtesy, but the rewards in effectiveness are unbelievable.

Let's take the toughest case—that of a young child of early school age. Does that child have the ability to articulate the feelings and intentions that adults would share while discussing a family problem? Not really. But the child has preferences when it comes to where to eat on a special day out, what television shows to watch, and so on. The family needs to use mealtimes and other more structured gatherings to list an agenda of things that need to be done and decisions that have to be discussed. When the question of "Who will do it?" arrives, the six-year-old candidate may be very well qualified and also quite willing. If it involves phoning to invite guests to a party or setting up the backyard, the person who is "in charge" must be set free to do it without constant meddling supervision, which effectively strips away the dignity of volunteering for the task. Yet in "chain of command" households, you will find that anybody can criticize, overrule, or otherwise harass anyone "beneath" them until they cannot complete any task and grow in responsibility. Sometimes the young enjoy volunteering when a parent says, "I need help getting ready for the picnic. Who would help me?" Children learn best and grow best when they have the adult coach alongside, turning responsibility over to them in small pieces.

Q. *But doesn't somebody have to have final responsibility for making a decision? Isn't that the man's place?*

A. Try talking through to agreement—consensus. Whenever a committee of two has to vote on an issue, it is a power move if one, "lords it over the other." It reveals that competition, not cooperation, is the driving force. Within the family, it is critical to bring everybody along and to give time to form agreement.

We learned a monumental lesson years ago when the Aldersgate Graded Curriculum Project was being launched. I was the general chair, and serious conflict emerged as we were hammering out some of the theological foundations on which this mutildenominational challenge was being launched. We had reached an impasse when we took our evening dinner break. Two Quaker women, representing the Evangelical Friends Alliance, came to me quietly and asked an insightful question: "Have you ever thought of making decisions by consensus, instead of voting? We do it that way in the Meeting." After dinner, I put the challenge to the entire six-denomination group. We decided we would find a way to agree without voting. Suddenly, the climate changed. Now, instead of "position speeches," everyone had to listen, not just wait for a turn to restate a position. We took no more votes in the entire project. We concluded that anything on which we could not reach clear consensus did not have to be decided at this time.

In a family, forced decisions that overpower objections often come at a very high price and are more a symptom of impatient pride and arrogance than of "final responsibility." Try consensus instead. Consensus does not mean agreement on everything. It means that everyone is heard and no one acts until the whole group is ready to act. Some members of the group may not have preferred the course of action that will be taken, but they reach a point where they are able to say, "OK, I can live with that."

10

"Head":
Another Name for Husband?

Paul Brand, surgeon among the lepers of India for a full missionary career, reflected theologically on his experiences as a surgeon. When he was a young student finishing his medical training, he observed some amazing facts about how "head" and "body" connect to each other.[1]

Two years of medical school had not prepared him for the day he was given his own cadaver head. He had chosen to trace the nerves from each of the "sensors"—the tongue, eyes, ears, and nose—into the brain. He needed to expose the nerve patterns to trace the pathways himself.

Brand said that seeing inside the human head was a revolutionary experience: "A whole person lies inside the bony box, locked in, protected, sealed away for the indispensable duties of managing one hundred trillion cells in a human body." He likened Jesus' departure from the infant church as the historical moment when His mission was "confined" into the Head so as to unite with the body, the church, to form one symphonic whole person—God present in the world!

Dr. Brand observed that the brain never "sees" in any literal sense: "If I opened one up to light, I would likely harm it irreparably." Nor does the brain "hear," but it is so cushioned that it only transforms reverberating sensations into the finest discriminations of sound. Nor does the brain experience any sense of "touch." Indeed, it has no tactile sense of its own, and may undergo surgical procedures without anesthesia. But the brain is

---

[1]Paul Brand and Philip Yancey, *In His Image* (Grand Rapids: Zondervan, 1984). See Chapters 10 and 11, "The Source," and "Confinement," pp. 120ff.

able to process touch sensations from the entire body and instantly detects the exact location of the pain, the pleasure, the tickling, or the burn.

While the cells of every human body undergo constant change, replacing themselves at least every seven years, the brain and nerve cells remain in place. They are always the same—the original equipment. And in these permanent cells, the identity of every person remains constant.

What a Head Does Best

There it is. In the New Testament metaphors of a marriage or of the church that use "head" and "body," the physiological analogy is explicit and inescapable:

The location of the head at the top of the body denotes less its "authority by position" than its utility in gathering the data from the entire body and utilizing the data to signal the body for appropriate action. The head functions like a periscope; it locates trouble, scouts terrain, and thus cares for the safety of the entire person. From this high lookout point, the head can sort out options. Then the head can empower the feet, legs, and torso to tilt and change direction to match decisions made on the basis of what is felt, seen, and heard.

The coordination of the entire body mass is a challenge thrust upon the head. The central nervous system, rooted as it is in the brain, brings data from the entire person into a synchronized and fully harmonious and coherent "whole." From this whole perception of the situation, the head coordinates all body potentials for flight or engagement with its environment. Only a fool could imagine that there would be any disagreement between head and body. "Who makes decisions" is irrelevant, because a head that does not respect the signals from the body could not survive. Since all messages from the body are processed as one person's data, this effective flow of data guarantees that the person's decisions are never handed down so as to ignore the body's contribution.

Hunger pangs, for example, are transmitted from the digestive system, but when danger arises, the body's cry for adrenaline to support fighting or fleeing prioritizes the body's actions in favor of survival. Hunger is postponed for the common good. The urgent demand of the excretory system is similarly encoded in the messages from the sigmoid colon or from the sphincter valve in the urinary tract. But these demands yield to culturally defined standards of privacy, even though the signals are acknowledged.

Eyes begin to search for a comfort station or rest stop sign, and the whole person is remarkably unified in decision and timing.

Head and body are one! Any argument about "who makes final decisions" is absurd. Schizophrenia—splitting the head from the body in some arrogant power struggle—becomes a painful and tragic pathology. Remember that the physiological metaphor of a husband and wife—"two become one"—is the continuous concept of Creation, Jesus, and St. Paul. The image reminds us of the remarkable mystery of Christ, the Head, and the church, His body. Any competitive pathology in marriage or in the union of Christ and church is an occasion to get help. And these remarkably powerful metaphors guide us in all Christian decision making.

The head is the identity feature of the total person. It includes the face, which we associate with the person. In naming the person, it is common for us to visualize the face of the person we hold in memory. As such, one-tenth of a person denotes the whole person. Transplant heads, and two people might escape detection for a fraud, since a criminal "lineup" focuses primarily on the faces. (Of course, fingerprints need to match the face, so the crime cannot escape detection when details are fully known.)

The head is the entry point for food. If the mouth takes in tainted food, the whole body suffers. If the body determines to expel the dangerous poison, it probably will exit through the head. But the head alone does not choose what is eaten. Many dieticians believe that the appetite picks up signals of deficiencies in the total body, cravings for foods that would balance out the mineral and nutritional needs of the body.

The head articulates. By encoding into language expressed as speech, the head becomes the primary organ of communication for the whole body. If a person is bound and gagged, or critically injured by a stroke or accident, body language must take over. The body can express basic urgent messages. "Body language" is the secondary communicating channel that verifies or contradicts the speech coming from the mouth.

The head is vulnerable. A blow to the head can immobilize the entire person. The principle that "head wounds are mortal" is both physiology and theology, as the serpent learned in Genesis 3:15. So the body instinctively defends the head—to throw up arms, to "duck" the head, and attempt to let the body take the major impact of a fall or a crash.

The head is naked. It is so fully active in its daily tasks that, except where the hair is meant to be, no part may be covered or clothed without impairing safety. It is exposed in severe weather of all kinds, doing its work with only the partial protection of a hat or cap or shielded beneath an umbrella—all calculated to allow the head to continue its scouting work in behalf of the whole person.

What a Head Needs Most

While a head might devise ideas, programs, or decisions, none of them will ever come into existence without full engagement of the body. If anyone wanted to find a metaphor denoting "mutuality," it would be hard to improve on the head-body metaphor. When hunger strikes, the hands or some other limbs must both prepare and feed the head. One young man we admire, born without arms, feeds himself with his feet, and washes his face and shaves with his feet.

The body makes up about 90 percent of the person's total weight and mass. The complicated skeleton, muscles, and vital organ structures pale beside the complexity of the brain. But in the body all of this mysterious self-maintaining ecosystem is at work. It is a magnificent mystery of God's creative ingenuity.

The body's activities to support life outnumber those of the head by about three to one. Some of the body's organs are paired, like lungs and kidneys, so that if one were lost through stroke or other tragedy, the other could sustain life. But life finally ends with the loss of the heart, liver, or digestive system.[2] An assassin usually attempts to strike a vital point in the upper body rather than hit the relatively smaller moving head.

The body supports the head. Think of the head as the treasured crown jewel held in place by the substantial body. Such a metaphor misses the genuine connection between that body and the head, but we can gain some useful insights from it:

The body is both the "gatherer" and the "distributor," compared to the "protector" role that the head fulfills. Although the head is more likely to do the external work, the workhorse is the body, which goes all day long at the most taxing pace. The woman of Proverbs 31:10–31 is a remarkable and classical "body" kind of a woman. As her husband sings his song of praise to this virtuous and mature woman, it is easy to imagine that he has sat at the gate in some official governing responsibility for the entire village, then returned home and found his wife exhausted. He listens to her report on buying property and the goods needed for the household. We can imagine

---

[2]The same is true, obviously, of the head. The brain is not replicated. Though severe loss of the function of one brain hemisphere may not end life, it profoundly impairs the whole body.

him admiring her and her day's accomplishments, celebrating them, but insisting that it is now time to stop the day's adventures and lie down to sleep. Both body and head must come to a time of peace and rest.

The body carries out its activities quietly, unobtrusively. The body does most of its silent and routine work behind the obscurity of clothing. Clothing hides from view the vital activities that are essential to the health of the whole person.

Reproduction occurs in the body. Here the conceiving, life-engendering miracle occurs. Here new life is formed and launched. The new person is umbilically attached to its mother, body to body, not head to head. Perhaps individuality requires this body-to-body launching, lest the parental image be so overpowering that it would prevent the new life from having an autonomous existence of its own.

Can you imagine a head without a body? Or a body without a head? We have walked with you through the obvious, even absurdly simple, characteristics of this head-body analogy. But we need to get the New Testament pictures straight. *Kephale* (head) and *soma* (body) invite us to contemplate the mystery of how "two become one."

Watch a Head at Work

In the string of head-body metaphors that St. Paul uses, none are more expansive than those in his arguments set down in 1 Corinthians 11:3. Look at it, strung out in separate images lines:

> I want you to know that
>> the head of every man is Christ,
>> the head of woman is man,
>> and the head of Christ is God.

Picture these head-body analogies this way if it helps:

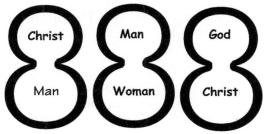

Notice that only God and woman are in single-category roles. Christ is "head" in one relationship and "body" in another. Man appears in both head and body positions. The pairings clearly denote how each of us may at the same time be in multiple relationship "systems," in which gifts and roles are for the common good and mission. Try picturing yourself in multiple systems. Here are some of ours:

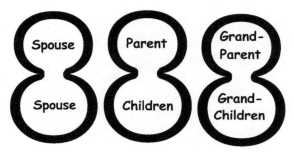

We also need to be aware of changing roles. We have recently executed an updated "Last Will and Testament," in which we have stipulated that certain circumstances will deliver durable power of attorney to our sons, so that they would become our protectors. We also included a succession to grandchildren, denoting their changing role in relationship to us.

Not long ago, I suggested in a sermon that if anyone thinks one's present role and responsibility are permanent, this experiment is worthwhile: "Look at the next multigenerational family gathering around your dinner table. Ask yourself, 'Among those around this table whose diapers have I changed?'" Then silently look at them again and tell yourself, 'They may one day be changing mine.'"

Watch a Head and a Body Shift Roles

We have watched now for several years as our friend Karen Carpenter has stood by her husband, Ellis. His spine was crushed while he was working on a home-repair mission project in Tennessee. Only a few months into their marriage, Karen stood by Ellis, first in Knoxville's Fort Sanders Presbyterian Hospital, then in Atlanta's Shepherd Spinal Center. Who knows how long the roles of "head" and "body" will be reversed? But it is clear in watching them that, although Ellis is immobilized, Karen is rising to the demand. In this profoundly deep relationship, there is enough flexibility to adapt to the new reality. It is clear that in a crisis, marital roles are reversible for the common good of the whole "persona" of the "two become one." The marriage vows call us to remember that, in sickness or in health, in plenty or in poverty, the mystery continues "till death do us part."

We saw this "role shift" all played out in the greatest drama of all time. A "Head" was determined to empower His "body" to take His place and carry on His work. We saw Him divest himself of heaven's status and authority, then enter into human life with its risks and limitations. He took the form of a servant leader, entering into a relationship of such intensity that the future of God's mission could be passed along to His disciples. We saw Jesus distribute authority and responsibility to this "body" without divorcing himself from the "body." The remarkable sequence of the transfer of authority is most powerfully reported in John 13–20. Jesus the "Head" took the servant role, submitting to care for this "body," which God was forming into the church. Read the remarkable account of the preparation for the final meal Jesus would share with the twelve apostles. Ponder the decisions Jesus made and the theological significance of what He did, as He switched roles symbolically, even before His crucifixion:

> ¹Now before the festival of the Passover, Jesus knew that his hour had come to depart from this world and go to the Father. Having loved his own who were in the world, he loved them to the end. ²The devil had already put it into the heart of Judas son of Simon Iscariot to betray him. And during supper ³Jesus, knowing that the Father had given all things into his hands, and that he had come from God and was going to God, ⁴got up from the table, took off his outer robe and tied a towel around himself. ⁵Then he poured water into a basin and began to wash the disciples' feet and to wipe them with the towel that was tied around him. (John 13:1–5, NRSV)

Underscore the middle sentence, which describes what Jesus did during supper. Here is a parable for all of us, but especially for men. If we would be servant leaders, we must become fully aware of the same three things Jesus "knew." Jesus knew (1) His calling and work, (2) where He came from, and (3) where He was going. This text describes Jesus' actions in the most profound defining issues for being a healthy person and having a clear sense of identity.

1. *Jesus knew His mission: "The Father had given all things into his hands."* Anyone who is grasping for power and control is an insecure and desperate person. Such a person believes that symbols of success and power are more important than seeing and doing what needs to be done. Such a person may be heard to exclaim, "I wouldn't be caught dead tryng

to unplug a toilet! That's janitor's work." Or, "Change a diaper? That's woman's work!" But anyone who is sure of his or her life's purpose can do anything that needs to be done. The mature individual is not so fragile as to imagine that "work determines worth." This person is truly free. You have seen a few such people, but they are rare. They are so at ease that they may embarrass you by their readiness to step in and perform some task that you might think is "beneath" them, simply because they knew somebody needed to do it.

Jesus was in such a situation at the Last Supper. People of wealth always provided a servant at the gate to wash everyone's feet. Guests arrived on foot, and their feet were often bloodied from road wear, always dusty in that era before paved roads. To "lie at table" around a common bowl placed on the floor meant to recline in a circle. Each guest rested on the left elbow, typically, dipping and eating with the right hand. This meant that each guest had to deal with the feet of the person to the left. The text suggests that Jesus knew that the disciples brought odors and unsanitary feet to the table. So Jesus "got up from the table" and did what somebody needed to do to improve the eating experience.

Jesus was a guest, just as they were, yet someone had to wash the feet. The disciples quite recently had been upset by one another's ambitions and rivalry over prized seats in the coming kingdom (Matt. 20:20–28). So they were in no mood to serve one another. The John 13 narrative says that Peter objects strenuously to Jesus' washing his feet. For some reason, Peter seems very uncomfortable with the reversal of roles. Some Bible scholars believe it had been Peter's responsibility to look after the foot cleansing at this meal, and that he forgot or refused to do it. Have you ever whined over an unwanted assignment, only to feel shame when the "teacher" did it for you?

2. *Jesus knew where He came from: "He had come from God."* A person's identity is deeply grounded in a sense of having a place in history, continuity with the past, and a connection to one's "roots." We might dismiss this as being irrelevant to us, because Jesus was uniquely "from God." But consider Jesus connections to His earthly parents. What stories had Jesus heard about His conception and birth? What was His relation to Joseph? What Sabbath blessings had Joseph and Mary pronounced over Him from infancy? These things had a powerful impact on His identity. Compare the narrative here—Jesus' self-composure to wash their feet—with insecure and often cruel "high achievers" you have

known. Did the high achievers miss the blessing[3] that connected them to their own history, giving them a sense of security and peace from which to operate in the corporate world? Occasionally, we hear confessions of men who are still trying to get their father's attention or to "prove I am worth loving." This second component of personal identity is worth checking out, if someone seems inflated with a sense of self-importance or achievement.

3. *Jesus knew where He was going: "He was going to God."* Jesus had a clear sense of destiny. Mature adults know the big picture, and keep their long-range goal in view to control the turbulence of day-by-day struggles on the way. Goals of achieving a fortune, of retiring, and of creating a life of comfort and ease do not serve anyone well. This third dimension of Jesus' healthy sense of identity is instructive to all of us. Both men and women, married and single, need to reexamine their long-term vision and destiny.

We have been associated with two or three major educational institutions. In each case, the fund-raising officials of those schools observed that people who settled their "Last Will and Testament" and designated the distribution of their remaining assets tended to live on and on and on! No wonder. Those donors are focused on a mission larger than life and more magnificent than their own small worlds of work and pleasure.

These three identity-profile indicators in Jesus are ideal for checking out who is really "safe," at a moral and spiritual level, to be a leader. Does the person have a clear calling and a secure vocation? Does the person have a clear sense both of vocation, of history, and of destiny? In His Great Commandment, Jesus calls us to

> Love the Lord your God
>> with all your soul, mind, and strength,
>> and your neighbor as yourself.

While the command is clearly a summons to obey, the final line is a simple statement of fact: We *will* love our neighbor as we love ourselves. People who have unfinished business with their vocation, with their

---

[3]Two wonderful books that deal with the importance of "blessing" in human relationships are Gary Smalley and John Trent, *The Blessing* (New York: Thomas Nelson, 1986) and Karl A. Olsson, *Come to the Party* (Dallas: Word Books, 1972). See also my own *Empower Your Kids to Be Adults: A Guide for Parents, Ministers, and Other Mentors* (Nappanee, Ind.: Evangel Publishing House, 2000).

personal history, or with their understanding of destiny are dangerous to be around if great responsibility falls on them. Have you ever seen an apparently competent person receive a promotion, then become a dangerous tyrant? Or have you seen an apparently amiable young person from an affluent home take on marriage and family responsibilities, only to turn into an abusive and careless person? Such people reveal that they have some unfinished "identity" business.

Since many of us marry during the adventure of trying to settle the three "identity" issues, we are likely to carry some competitive—even violent—behavior into our marriages. Jesus offers us a model of maturity, and its most visible feature is servant-submission. In John 13, Jesus even turns the spotlight on the footwashing episode:

> [12]After he had washed their feet, had put on his robe, and had returned to the table, he said to them, "Do you know what I have done to you? [13]You call me Teacher and Lord—and you are right, for that is what I am. [14]So if I, your Lord and Teacher, have washed your feet, you also ought to wash one another's feet. [15]For I have set you an example, that you also should do as I have done to you. [16]Very truly, I tell you, servants are not greater than their master, nor are messengers greater than the one who sent them. [17]If you know these things, you are blessed if you do them." (John 13:12–17, NRSV)

Jesus accepts intimate vulnerability, made safe by His long-range hope. He immediately announces that He will be betrayed by one from the circle, but seals it with: "Love one another; as I have loved you, that you also love one another" (John 13:34). All of this teaching is wrapped in His vision of a reunion in "Father's house." An amazing description of the future life in intimate community unfolds in John 14.

Jesus transforms servant-submission into a level-field community. Having accepted the responsibility of being a "Head" who lives by servant-submission, Jesus inducts the remaining eleven disciples into a community of peers:

> [12]This is my commandment, that you love one another as I have loved you. [13]No one has greater love than this, to lay down one's life for one's friends. You are my friends if you do what I

command you. ¹⁵I do not call you servants any longer, because the servant does not know what the master is doing; but I have called you friends, because I have made known to you everything that I have heard from my Father. ¹⁶You did not choose me but I chose you. And I appointed you to go and bear fruit, fruit that will last, so that the Father will give you whatever you ask him in my name. ¹⁷I am giving you these commands so that you may love one another. (John 15:12–17, NRSV).

His teaching about the Holy Spirit continues through John 16, then a full chapter is devoted to Jesus' prayer "that they may be one, just as We are" (17:22). The betrayal and Crucifixion are reported in chapters 18 and 19. But in John 20, the Resurrection brings a reunion between Jesus and His followers. Jesus appears to the apostles, huddled behind locked doors. In that unlikely setting, Jesus makes the final distribution of His authority as "Head." He charges the apostles with continuing the legacy of the "bride." Look at that transfer of authority:

²⁰He showed them his hands and his side. Then the disciples rejoiced when they saw the Lord. ²¹Jesus said to them again, "Peace be with you. As the Father has sent me, so I send You." ²²When he had said this, he breathed on them and said to them, "Receive the Holy Spirit. ²³If you forgive the sins of any, they are forgiven them; if you retain the sins of any, they are retained." (John 20:20–23, NRSV)

Here the "head" forms the "body" and invests His "breath," the Holy Spirit, in the life of the continuing community of faith. God's original breathing of the breath of life into the First Adam is paralleled here by the Last Adam's breathing upon His disciples. Both Adams seized the opportunity to invest the "bride" with dominion and authority.

Perhaps these images will get us back on track in our marriages and in our congregations. The original Adam was split into the original Bride and Groom, and by that physiological metaphor God denoted that specific gifts belong to each. Here the second Adam predicts another split between Groom and bride, as Jesus ascends and leaves the bride to do her work in the world. The final consummation of all things will bring the Groom back to the bride dressed in white, surrounded by the hosts of us who are "in Christ."

Husbands as Heads

So in what sense is the husband "head" of a marriage? If physiology is a metaphor for marriage and for the structure of the church, then surely we can speculate about possible implications. But let us not forget that the tragic mark of sin persists, creeping in to separate us from our Creation goal. Jesus died to "put things right," but we still stand under the terrible cloud of the tragedy of the Fall and the sinful tendencies predicted in Genesis 3.

Husbands are endowed with musculature, hormones, and instincts to protect, to surround, and to express affection through the acquisition of food and wealth from the outer world.[4] Even by the unique mapping capabilities of the male brain, husbands are experts at tasks of looking out, sighting potential danger or havens of peace, finding the way there, and making it home again.[5]

As a result of the androgen bath in the fetal brain between the sixteenth and twenty-sixth weeks of development, males have specialized optic systems with excellent three-dimensional perception. Males are less likely to walk into hanging objects from fences or trees, for example, suggesting that their eyes are favorably equipped for moving through irregular visual fields. Females often have difficulty identifying the distance to a clothesline unless a vertical object such as a clothespin is on the line. Males' brains are generally better equipped than females' brains to do transformational logic, which depends on formal operational thought and problem solving. Such challenges require three-dimensional reasoning, and males' perceptual skills seem to transfer to some of these mathematical and engineering challenges.[6]

---

[4]Basic body differences, including that of musculature, are explored in several popularly written articles on sex differences. These typically cite interviews with the primary researchers, with generous quotations. See for example Pamela Weintraub, "The Brain: His and Hers," *Discover*, April 1981, pp. 15ff. See also Jo Durden-Smith, "Male and Female—Why?" *Quest/80*, October 1980, pp. 55 ff.

[5]See also David Gelman, "Just How the Sexes Differ," *Newsweek*, May 18, 1981, pp. 172 ff. This and other reports focus on the "spatial" or mapping sense that seems to excel in males.

[6]Dianne McGuinness, "How Schools Discriminate Against Boys," *Human Nature* (February 1979), 82–88, reports very different uses and skills related to vision comparing boys to girls, including likely connections between three-dimensional depth perception and higher mathematical operations.

Taken as a group, men tend to be more assertive and aggressive than wives and women in general. Even the most introverted male, if he has a healthy sense of identity, "takes over" in the outer world. He negotiates, protects, and is ready to intervene for wife and children. But if even an extroverted male is insecure as to his identity, history, destiny, or vocation, that healthy assertive pattern can be diminished or even inverted into depression, addiction, and irresponsibility.

Husbands are observer-referees. Their periscopic gift is also expressed in objectivity. At their best, they are arbiters of justice, slicing through conflicts and hurts to settle issues in the family and the community. Indeed, their objectivity tends to insulate them from feelings to such an extent that they tend to try to "solve" everything within hearing distance. "But we don't want you try to fix everything all the time," wives and children may complain. "We just want you to listen to us." Remember that the specialization of the male brain late in fetal development shrinks the corpus callosum by 25 million fibers. This reduces the impact of the right hemisphere (feelings) on the left hemisphere (decision making). In an emergency, a male can block out risks and emotions to make an instant analysis and decision. On the other hand, tell a man a story, and he is less likely to analyze it. Story and music go to a male's right hemisphere, where moral values and beliefs are stored. Jesus never taught without a parable, and Nathan the prophet confronted King David with a story about a poor man whose only sheep was taken by a rich neighbor, who wanted to prepared a meal for a guest. "You are that man!" Nathan announced after the king had passed judgment based on the story.

No doubt the "differentiated" list could go on and on. It is enough if we can see that anatomy and physiology establish some intrinsic differences that equip males to present specialized gifts to their marriages and their communities. It is tragic, however, that these same gifts, when driven by insecurity, can become tools of abuse and violence. Such exploitive behaviors are under God's judgment, of course, but they also come under the canopy of God's grace as targets for His healing and transformation. Those of us men who suffer from feelings of inferiority are good candidates for healing and wholeness in the community of faith.

What emerge when we study male physiology, are the male gifts that stand behind the popular stereotypes. If we can see male behavior patterns as expressions of potential, a gift instead of cultural baggage, we may be on our way to synchronizing our marriages and our male-female relationships based on respect, instead of on labeling or on competition. Men should cut the nerve of the Marlboro man stereotype, setting them free to be "real men" in the gentlest, respect-based roles they can develop. By the same token, women should end the assault on masculine stereotypes, which are merely caricatures rooted in physiology.

Healthy husbands are submissive servants, fully committed to protect, support, and care for those they love—even at the cost of laying down their health and their very lives. Jesus did for His bride, the church!

Where There Is a Deadhead

In most cultures, husbands are the "family identity." Lose or change "heads" and the surviving family undergoes major, often traumatic disruption.

We visited the hospital where our friend Glenn lay comatose. A severe head injury in a car crash had been treated and death averted, but the vital signs predicted no recovery of consciousness. Glenn was a recently graduated high-school athlete. There was not a single mark on his well-formed body. Only the neck had been broken. But across the months, we watched the body soften, beginning its slow degenerative process.

Glenn's body simply could not replace the critical functions of the head, but the loss was not simply to the head. The body was dying, too. So also, marriages with a dysfunctional head are haunted by a slow but certain atrophy and death. A congregation whose "head" is a deformed version of Christ the head is likely to become a dysfunctional body.

We commonly describe a person as being "wrongheaded" about lifestyle, about diet, or about some belief. Perhaps that metaphor signals the fact that we need to check our "body" and "head" relationships. To become "right headed" might mean to recognize the true and healthy "Head" available to us. When we say, "Christ is the Head of this home, " that may be the first step toward a reorganization of our marriages. And when Christ is not the Head of the family, the husband likely will have a hard time fulling the servant-submission responsibilities that come with the territory of being regarded as "head" by wife and children.

Dorothy Sayers outlined in her *Mind of the Maker* three aspects of what she calls the "humiliation of God." First, God stooped to meet us in the Incarnation, by which Jesus was stripped of the privileges of deity and entered into our human existence. Second, in the Crucifixion, God became sin for us and took its consequences of death. But Sayers observes that the greatest humiliation of God was the third: God chose to express His divine

Person on earth through embarrassingly imperfect humans, and He calls us His body.

The life of any body depends on attachment to the right head. In the case of Jesus, the Lord of the church, health of the Body is assured only if we stay connected to the Head. Only He can breathe on us and infuse us with His Spirit—bringing life, harmony, and wholeness.

In much the same way, every husband finds that his wife and children win him the widest reputation: they are his truest expression. He depends on his family more than he knows. His only hope is that there is no dysfunctional connection between body and head, leaving him morally or spiritually comatose in a world where so much needs yet to be done, a world that calls him to be a "whole person."

In this chapter, we have explored the simplest possible interpretation of the basic "head" and "body" metaphor, which the New Testament uses to describe both Christ/church and husband/wife relationships. In the next chapter, we will look at the distinct metaphor of "body" to continue that exploration.

Questions People Ask

Q. *You seem to suggest that males automatically do masculine things and females automatically do feminine things. Doesn't this take us back to the old traditional male-female roles?*

A. We want to expose the unthinking stereotypes of males and females. I had an opportunity to lead a Bible study with thirty officers inside the Pentagon in the mid-nineties. They were facing policy challenges that troubled many of them. I offered them the New Testament texts describing polar opposites in males. To illustrate, I set the apostle John in contrast to John the Baptist. Then I observed that American culture in general, and military culture in particular, were suffering from too narrow a definition of masculinity. Basically, we have created the image of the "macho" male, and that was contributing to some conclusions among kinder and gentler males about their suitability to occupy clear masculine roles. I appealed for these officers to rewrite the Code of Miliary Conduct to honor this wide spectrum of male potentials. Among other points, I speculated that the gentle apostle John likely was left-handed, perhaps a poet and a musician. I noted that he was respected and trusted both by Jesus and by the remaining apostle group. When the meeting ended, I was greeted by a general who is a flutist, an admiral who is a concert pianist, and a joint-chiefs general who is a cellist.

When this kinder-gentler correction is made, an intrinsic male giftedness still comes through. In this chapter, we have attempted to celebrate that. Women who are executive administrators can lead corporations effectively, representing a neglected end of the spectrum now open for women. In the same way the intrinsic gifts of the female tend to baffle anyone who would stereotype them as being outside the gift package that is a woman. (We will turn to those gifts in Chapter 11.)

Q. *You use a term that eludes me. What is a "Marlboro man?"*

A. Marlborough Cigarettes, when they were first introduced, attracted a very small group of customers, mostly university graduates. After all, who else knew how to spell or even pronounce the name? A market research report urged two things: Change the spelling of the name to make it simpler (Marlboro). Evoke an image of toughness and macho masculinity, since men tend to be an important part of the cigarette consumption population. So "Marlboro" became the spelling of the name and an unshaved, tough cowboy with a desert-tough environment at the backdrop became the image. We use the term therefore to mean an intentionally exaggerated and deformed set of male behaviors, designed to emphasize "tough" masculinity.

11

"Body":
Another Name for Wives?

Myron was perhaps four or five years older than I was. In our thinly populated farming community in Kansas, everybody knew Myron. When any of us visited Myron's home, we quickly forgot any pity we might have brought because of Myron's severe disabling conditions. Early in life, he had mastered the imaginative engineering skills of the Erector Set. This toy was all made of metal parts from which to construct toys or anything you could imagine—much as children today do with Legos. Myron was also a master at shortwave radio communication, and he was making audio recordings well ahead of any of the rest of us. Myron was home-schooled long before it was fashionable, because public schools were unable to deal with Myron's severe physical impairments. As a result, Myron mastered things other schoolboys rarely dreamed of trying.

This impressive genius was housed in a body that jerked intermittently and involuntarily with severe spasms. His head was uncertainly balanced, bobbing irregularly, and his speech was difficult to understand. Myron's hands worked only with enormous concentration and effort, which caused muscular twitches and distortions in his face.

I thought of Myron when reading Dr. Paul Brand's review of a televised meeting of two young people with cerebral palsy. One of them, a young man, had made astonishing progress. He could spell out words using foot gestures on the floor. He could activate a typewriter by using his toe to trigger a gadget connected to the specific keys. The other television guest, a young woman, had been placed in a mental hospital because no other Ohio agency had facilities for her extended care.

The young woman, like her male counterpart, made involuntary facial grimaces, drooled, and was in every way cataleptic. She had had no rehabilitation therapy except for a large wall chart divided into eighty squares with stems and completions for her ideas. When asked whether she had any questions for the young man, she convulsed, eyes dancing. A volunteer from her hospital read her eyes as she communicated through her chart. Nearly five minutes later, she had asked her question: "Were . . . you . . . angry?"[1]

No doubt the parents and brothers of my friend Myron heard and read his bodily gestures of anger and frustration. When Myron's parents died, he found himself in a nursing home. I have shuddered to think that his care may have deteriorated to match that of the Ohio girl. His disabilities were so visible as to cause many people to assume he could not possibly think or feel what others think or feel. Yet I doubt that our community has produced a brighter son.

I tell Myron's story because I want to underscore Paul Brand's observation that the head and the body depend on each other more than we may imagine. And since "head and body" are St. Paul's metaphors for what husband and wife bring to marriage, we need to explore what he means by the "body," because that metaphor is consistently used in Paul's letters as a reference to the woman. He says that the church is the "body of Christ," the "bride." If that metaphor can rise on the horizon of our growing understanding, we will celebrate here the elegance of "body" as another name for womanly gifts in general and for wifely gifts in particular.

What a Body Does Best

The body is about 95 percent of a person's total physical mass. Yet when I hand my camera to someone to shoot a photo of Robbie and me, I keep coaching the photographer to move in close. I find myself saying, "Don't worry about the feet. Get our faces up close." Lopping off lower body parts is common in photography.

Yet the body does most of the work. An able-bodied person is one who has no disability. Effective use of the hands and feet commonly guarantees that a person can learn to perform virtually any task. Indeed, for most of human history, most work has been done "by hand," and many human

---

[1]Brand and Yancey, *In His Image*, 141.

accomplishments are measured in "feet." "Handmade" long was the only means of production. Today, the term denotes either necessity or first-quality custom work.

Not only are hands and feet features of the body, but the heavy-duty processes of digestion, respiration, circulation, reproduction, and excretion are carried on by the complicated working of the body.[2] Our bodies are so valued that they are shrouded (clothed) to keep them from being injured or exploited. "Naked, but unashamed" (Gen. 2:25) denotes the exception—the marriage environment where transparency and full trust keep us safe. But in the rest of the world, we keep our bodies clothed.

Even so, it is impossible to think of a body without a head attached to it, to synchronize every body need and feeling. We should analyze carefully the "head-body" metaphor because the New Testament's use of these images has been so badly abused. We can celebrate the complete interdependence of "head and body" in our own sense of self. Since we are fallen and deformed men and women, we need help in discarding the nonsense about Chief Executive Officer ("Head") versus subservient inferior employee ("body"). These distortions of the head-body analogy have contaminated even our ways of reading Scripture. God's original design for couples was, "Let them have dominion" (Gen. 1:26). Sovereignty is one face of the image of God given to both men and women. So marriage is all the more a mystery: "two become one!"

What a Body Needs Most

Robbie and I once visited a family friend named Glenn who was comatose as the result of a severe head injury in an auto crash. Glenn had recently graduated from high school, where he had been a fine athlete. There was not a mark on that well-formed body laid in the intensive care unit; only the head was injured. But across the following months, we watched the muscles of the body soften and begin the slow degenerative process toward death. Such an accident emphasizes the pathos of any impairment between head and body. Connectedness and synchrony are essential for any person's well-being and effectiveness.

The head is the center of the nervous system that spreads throughout the body. The head, with its neurological symphony playing endlessly, is not

---

[2] See the section, "What a Head Needs Most" in Chapter 10, where we develop more fully some of the "body" gifts.

isolated in a white bone box as the "top appendage" of the body. It is omnipresent in the body, down to the end joint of the smallest finger or toe. The nerves while technically in the body, are in fact extensions of the brain. Tom Michalko, whom I described in *Bonding: Relationships in the Image of God* [3] as one of two anonymous cases of "anomalous dominance" brain organization cases, survived a head-on crash with a gravel truck in the week he was scheduled to graduate from Asbury Seminary. Tom's blow, sustained to the front of the right brain hemisphere, put him into a deep coma. When I received the call about his accident, I relayed word to the entire cast of players in our brown-bag weekly lunch group. We gathered at the University of Kentucky's emergency unit while a neurosurgeon checked Tom's "head-body" connections. We would not see Tom's eyes open for nearly ten days, but in those first hours before immobilizing Tom for treatment, the neurosurgeon checked him out. As the doctor pinched his extremities, Tom would slap the irritated area, consistently following the doctor's checkpoints. In spite of a major concussion, a fractured vertebra in the neck, a broken left leg, and a complete shattering of the facial bone structure, Tom's reactions assured us that the prognosis for recovery was good.

The head contains the major sense centers for collecting data essential to the body's safety and movement. This "periscope" is conveniently hoisted by the body to a position of vulnerability, but one of impressively fine perspective. From this periscopic vantage point the head faithfully signals the body to protect the whole person: *See that broken pavement! Shift right!* the brain says. At the same time, the body is giving important feedback to the head about the whole person's comfort and need: hunger, thirst, heat or cold. Aside from hat, goggles, and earmuffs that one might wear, the head remains largely exposed to weather and other hazards.

The head also is the major transmitter of personal messages. The mouth broadcasts not only what the head thinks, but also what the body reports out. Except in rare cases of low self-respect or shame, the face remains uncovered. So "facial language" typically gives a person's secrets away. Once while lecturing at a university in Michigan, I read pain on Robbie's face. The pain had persisted three weeks in spite of two medical visits and a round of antibiotics. What she was unwilling to tell me about her severe abdominal pain was clearly visible on her face. I was intent on getting a diagnosis, even if it meant a series of separate tests for the appendix, ovaries, kidneys, and

---

[3] *Bonding: Relationships in the Image of God*, 72 ff., "Differentiating the Adam Brain."

colon. Back at our guest house, while packing to load the car, I plied her with questions about her pain. I then announced that we were canceling our plans for a three-day vacation to Niagara Falls. We needed to return to Kentucky so that Robbie could have medical consultations and tests. This much pain was too much, and it was being telegraphed from her body to her face.

The New Testament "head-body" metaphor is impossible to miss: Neither head nor body is viable alone. For either to become adversary to the other reduces the person to a spastic, convulsive condition. Heads that ignore bodies are in big trouble, and bodies that cut off their heads for spite have ended their own well-being.

Watch a Body at Work

Since "head-body" is primarily St. Paul's metaphor in Scripture, it is only right to let him show us how the body works. Remember that Paul employs a double metaphor in Ephesians to let the "head-body" image represent two mysteries: the relationship between Christ and the church, and the relationship between a husband and a wife. St. Paul has no interest in making two statements exactly the same, so he uses his metaphor with some fluidity. In Ephesians 5, Christ is Head and the church is body, requiring both to serve in separate roles. But in 1 Corinthians 12, Paul cites features of both the head and the body in the church. He finally says, "Now you are the body of Christ, and each one of you is a part of it." Here in 1 Corinthians 12, that "body" includes eyes and ears.

In 1 Corinthians 12, Paul is trying to establish a coherent picture of how the Holy Spirit's gifts fit together for the common good of the faith community:

> [4]There are different kinds of gifts, but the same Spirit. [5]There are different kinds of service, but the same Lord. [6]There are different kinds of working, but the same God works all of them in all men. . . .

> [12]The body is a unit, though it is made up of many parts; and though all its parts are many, they form one body. So it is with Christ. [13]For we were all baptized by one Spirit into one body—whether Jews or Greeks, slave or free—and we were all given the one Spirit to drink. (1 Cor. 12:4–6, 12–13, NIV)

How more eloquently could anyone describe the mutual dependency and symphonic unity of marriage or of a faith community? More provocatively, Paul goes on to describe conflict, paralysis, and spastic body life caused by domineering body parts that "put down" the others:

> [14]Now the body is not made up of one part but of many. [15]If the foot should say, "Because I am not a hand, I do not belong to the body," it would not for that reason cease to be part of the body. [16]And if the ear should say, "Because I am not an eye, I do not belong to the body," it would not for that reason cease to be part of the body. [17]If the whole body were an eye, where would the sense of hearing be? If the whole body were an ear, where would the sense of smell be? [18]But in fact God has arranged the parts in the body, every one of them, just as he wanted them to be. [19]If they were all one part, where would the body be? [20]As it is, there are many parts, but one body. (1 Cor. 12:14–20, NIV).

And what does our treatment of our bodies tell us about where we place the real honor and deference? Which gets the lion's share of the clothing budget—head or body? And why?

> [21]The eye cannot say to the hand, "I don't need you!" And the head cannot say to the feet, "I don't need you!" [22]On the contrary, those parts of the body that seem to be weaker are indispensable, [23]and the parts that we think are less honorable we treat with special honor. And the parts that are unpresentable are treated with special modesty, [24]while our presentable parts need no special treatment. But God has combined the members of the body and has given the greater honor to the parts that lacked it, [25]so that there should be no division in the body, but that its parts should have equal concern for each other. [26]If one part suffers every part suffers with it; if one part is honored, every part rejoices with it. (1 Cor. 12:21–26, NIV).

There it is again! Everywhere the head-body metaphor denotes co-regency, joint tenancy, and shared birthright: "Its parts . . . have equal concern for each other." Suffering or celebration affects the whole person, not just the part being attacked or honored.

> [27]Now you are the body of Christ, and each one of you is part of it. [28]And in the church God has appointed first of all apostles, second prophets, third teachers, then workers of miracles, also those having gifts of healing, those able to help others those with gifts of administration, and those speaking in different kinds of tongues. [29]Are all apostles? Are all prophets? Are all teachers? Do all work miracles? [30]Do all have gifts of healing? Do all speak in tongues? Do all interpret? [31]But eagerly desire the greater gifts. And now I will show you the most excellent way. (1 Cor. 12:27–30, NIV)

Paul goes on to define the "way of love" (or "charity," as the King James Version calls it). This absolute equal concern for each other that he describes in 12:25 is amplified by the entire content of 1 Corinthians 13, where he details the behavior of love, the "most excellent way."

"You are the body of Christ," Paul tells his Christian sisters and brothers. Christ directs the church, just as the human head must direct the human body. The common value of the various gifts within the body adds up to the enormous potential of a healthy body connected to Christ, its head. And so we have no trouble turning from the Ephesians 5 metaphors of head and body back to the 1 Corinthians definitions, where we see that the husband-wife relationship is clarified and corrected by these images as well.

Wives as Bodies

As we noted earlier, physiology is used as an analogy to unlock a theological mystery. How are wives to be understood, valued, and appreciated in light or the metaphor of "body?" For that matter, how are women in the faith community enhanced and treasured, when we consider that they are ever-present reminders of our common identity, as "the body of Christ?"

Women are, in fact, "bodies." Even in their most demeaning moments, males will refer to a beautiful woman as "a body." Perhaps that is an admission of complexity of womanhood, because men recognize that woman does not have detached sexual parts—she is intrinsically woman. "What a body!" may be exploitive, but it is also the lowest form of theology.

A woman appeals to a man for deeper reasons than either likely knows. From Eden until now, males "leave father and mother" and follow the females' attraction until they "cleave to" a woman whom they know to be at one with themselves—either in holy mystery or in earthly blasphemy. Men have to accept the fact that they move from one dependency to anther. How helpless and hopeless is all of that bravado, unless men find the mystery of "two become one"?

Women are endowed with more complex, more integrated perceptual abilities than are men. Perhaps because of their globally integrated brain structure,[4] women are able to reason more intuitively compared to men's more typically split-brain linear and analytic reasoning. Intuitive thinking is lightning quick and requires access to the right-brain hemisphere. Some left-handed men are gifted in intuitive reasoning as well, and the left-handed men who are artists and musicians are examples of this connection between right-hemisphere dominance and intuitive gifts. All of us would use intuitive reasoning if we had full access to the brain resources for it, because it is generally faster and more accurate than abstract logical reasoning. One wrong piece of data in a logical calculation yields a completely wrong conclusion. But with intuitive, nonverbal, global thinking, the data considered for a decision include past experiences, impressions, attitudinal readings, and many other perceptions that do not translate into language or numbers. The intuitive judgment collects all of these data and spins off an almost instant reading that is astonishingly reliable.[5]

As is so often the case, our greatest gifts may make us vulnerable to having those gifts exploited. Women's potential for sensing people's needs and rising to take care of them can be badly violated when men reduce them to menial and trivial tasks, or exploit them in other ways. Women live for other people! Taken as a group, women more often make decisions on the basis of "how it will affect everyone involved." While men are "objective-referee" types, women tend to be "subjective-concerned" people. This subjective gift can show up as an undue concern for "keeping up appearances" because of "what people think," but also as genuine pity for people in trouble. The strength of a woman's "people concern" is obvious as a wife looks after the needs of the entire family, including the husband. More than the husband

---

[4]*Bonding: Relationships in the Image of God*, 72ff.

[5]See McGuinness, "How Schools Discriminate Against Boys," 82–88, and Weintraub, "The Brain: His and Hers," 15 ff. Both articles were cited in previous chapters

himself, she is likely to be sensitive to his health and physical welfare. She typically knows better than he when he needs a holiday. And her gift of sensing what others feel may extend to the widest circle of contacts. No wonder Jesus called the church His "body," given the mission of the Christian faith—to wrap arms of compassion around the innocent, the poor, the wounded, the sinners, and the dying.

What emerges in the New Testament's image of wives as "bodies" is the clear picture of the selfless gift of strength, support, and concern they bring to every situation—within the family and beyond. Healthy wives, as well as husbands, voluntarily "submit to one another." They enter into the passions, celebrations, and griefs of the mate's vocations, dreams, and hopes. The "head" and "body" of Ephesians submit to one another out of reverence for Christ."

In this chapter we have looked more closely at the "body" part of the "head-body" metaphor of the New Testament. We want you to keep a focus on "body as wife." We want to discount false images of "submission," which suggest that only women are obligated to submit to their spouses. The submission text opens with a command to mutual respect and submission: "Submit to one another out of reverence for Christ." Unilateral submission is nowhere taught in Scripture. Wherever it is demanded by men, it treats women as being inferior and passive. It is exhilarating to see St. Paul's more complete description of how the body works—as a unity, with absolute mutual respect and mutual experience. This concept rests squarely on Creation's command in Genesis 1: "Let them have dominion." God said, "Let them rule" over the created universe. So this insight is our gift to you here.

Questions People Ask

Q. *You suggest that the metaphor of husband and wife as "head" and "body" in a "whole-person" model of a marriage means that both partners need to be well coordinated and not "spastic," with some disorder that disables the husband-wife relationship. What would such a neurologically damaged marriage look like?*

A. Think of a marriage you know well in which the husband does not "read" the needs and longings of the wife. That is a spastic marriage. The "whole-person" marriage is one in which respect and mutual dependency are so spontaneous that the two partners communicate and make decisions as one.

In another scenario, picture a wife who is emotionally unable to telegraph clear data to her husband, the head. Perhaps the wife is mentally ill, caught in an addiction, or carries symptoms of sexual abuse during childhood. The healthy husband's love and commitment will care for her needs and will accept the challenges of discovering those needs alone. He will desperately search for help and healing resources for his wife—to the neglect of lesser priorities of work, recreation, even worship.

One could switch head and body roles here and extend the examples further. We are watching a husband leave his ministry vocation because caring for his Alzheimer-seized wife has become his total focus. Twenty years ago we witnessed a wife who rearranged her life to "cover all bases" after her husband was injured in a mission construction accident, leaving him a paraplegic. You may think of other marriage situations that demonstrated a major breakdown between "head and body." Those situations underscore the miracle of "two become one."

Q. How do you suggest that I cope with a husband who believes he is following the Bible when he functions as a lone ranger, authoritarian-type "head of the house?"

A. Some women quietly ignore the control strategies that an authoritarian husband uses. Others draw a line in the sand and "separate the powers," establishing their own ways of using the power that is out of reach of their husbands. The fact is this: Neither a man nor a woman is independent of the other, and if their marriage continues, they will come to depend increasingly on each other.

On the other hand, if your husband begins listening to you, reading your needs and longings, and depending on your perceptions as he makes his personal decisions, you can walk with him into a "mystery of two become one" marriage. Jesus' principle that we should "overcome evil with good" can change any relationship.

But this does not mean staying in an abusive marriage. If your husband is physically or verbally abusive, it is urgent for you to get help. Ask him to join you in this search for a way of living respectfully and working together in your home. If you are in a congregation that teaches a "chain of command" model of marriage, you will need to search for better biblical counseling than you may find there.

Q. My wife and I have been in this church for more than twenty years and we raised our children here. Now they are grown, and we have grown increasingly uncomfortable with the hierarchical model we have been taught here, even though it is supposedly based on the Bible. You cannot imagine how we have needed your teaching on the Creation model for men and women. We were always afraid to think of seeking another church home because we were afraid of "leaving the Bible behind." We always suspected that the "chain of command" teaching was off base, because in our best times we never lived that way in our marriage or home. We have really been "two become one" all along. What shall we say to our adult children, who now have "chain of command" marriages?

A. It is never too late to speak the truth. Your children deserve to hear your story, including the account of your discomfort with this teaching all along. Trust your adult kids! They have watched you and know your marriage better than any outsiders. And trust their intelligence. As honest parents, do not demand that they see what you see, but encourage them to be honest in their reading of Scripture. Your only apology, if it is one, is that you didn't find a way to discuss your discomfort sooner.

12

The New Adam:
From Image to Likeness

When Eugene O'Neill put theological lines in the mouth of his main character in *The Great God Brown*, he stumbled intuitively on what many of us have been observing over a lifetime. Let me paraphrase to make his lines include all of us:

> This is Daddy's bedtime secret for today:
> Humans are born broken.
> We spend our lives mending.
> The grace of God is the glue![1]

Life is a pilgrimage of one kind or another. Without question, we are all imprinted with God's image, which gives us an enormous potentiality. But we are also flawed. We have deformed ideas about ourselves and about other people. We are egocentric and imagine ourselves at the center of the universe. This self-centered vision puts us into deformed relationships. A marriage that brings together two egocentric people will have conflict, competition, and a win-or-lose complex hanging over much of the relationship. Still, the participants carry God's image. They have a sense of justice, an awareness of good and evil, and the power of moral choice. They represent God within the earthly Creation. But even with that moral endowment they may descend into increasingly violent, abusive, and

---

[1]Paraphrased from Eugene O'Neill, "The Great God Brown," act 4, scene 1.

destructive patterns of choice and life. On the other hand, they may become increasingly reflective and aware of their own tendency to be self-centered. They may become increasingly penitent before the God whose image they bear. These folks will be open to grace and the transformation that Jesus, the Second Adam, can bring. In short, they are being transformed into the likeness of God, and the basic *imago Dei* is the raw material with which God's grace is at work, sanctifying them and moving them in the trajectory toward wholeness.

A Story of Reflection and Transformation

Working as we do within a developmental and a transformational perspective, Robbie and I are always seeing patterns of pilgrimage in people's life stories. Today at breakfast, Brian told us the story of his transformation. As a college freshman at a Colorado public university, he "dropped into the hole of life," he said. We asked him whether he was spelling that whole or hole. He smiled and rushed ahead with his story. Transferring to Greenville College, his dad's alma mater, he became angry and disorderly. In desperation, he gathered three other rebels together and they started a Bible study where they expressed their cynicism. Within a semester, the Bible-study group had expanded to more than two dozen. (We thought of John Westerhoff's thesis that we need to " baptize doubt" and give our young adults a "blessing" to pursue truth vigorously and with a hermeneutic of suspicion.) So Brian came to faith that way. He is now getting married and will return after the honeymoon to continue his study for pastoral ministry with us.

In another century, John Wesley was a classical example of the O'Neill pattern of being born broken and spending one's life mending, with God's grace as the glue. Since John Wesley kept a journal, he prepared himself for reflection, which is an essential prerequisite to transformation. Here are lines lifted from the published version of Wesley's *Journal*. The entries are all written with the reflection of a lifetime behind him:

> I believe, till I was about ten years old, I had not sinned away that "washing of the Holy Ghost" which was given me in baptism; having been strictly educated and carefully taught that I could only be saved "by universal obedience, by keeping all the commandments of God"; in the meaning of which I was diligently instructed. And those instructions, so far as they

respected outward duties and sins, I gladly received and often thought of. But all that was said to me of inward obedience or holiness I neither understood nor remembered. So that I was indeed as ignorant of the true meaning of the law as I was of the gospel of Christ.

The next six or seven years (ages 11–17) were spent at school; where outward restraints being removed, I was much more negligent than before, even outward duties, and almost continually guilty of outward sins, which I knew to be such, though they were not scandalous in the eye of the world. However, I still read the Scriptures, and said my prayers morning and evening. And what I now hoped to be saved by, was (1) not being so bad as other people; (2) having still a kindness for religion; and (3) reading the Bible, going to church, and saying my prayers.

Being removed to the University for five years (to about age 22), I still said my prayers both in public and in private, and read, with the Scriptures, several other books of religion, especially comments on the New Testament. Yet I had not all this while so much as a noting of inward holiness; nay, went on habitually, and for the most part very contentedly, in some or other known sin: indeed, with some intermission and short struggles, especially before and after the holy Communion, which I was obliged to receive thrice a year. I cannot well tell what I hoped to be saved by now, when I was continually sinning against that little light I had; unless by those transient fits of what many divines taught me to call repentance.

When I was about twenty-two, my father pressed me to enter into holy orders [licensing toward ordination]. At the same time, the providence of God directed me to Kempis's Christian Pattern. I began to see that true religion was seated in the heart and that God's law extended to all our thoughts, as well as words and actions. I was, however, very angry at Kempis for being too strict; though I read him only in Dean Stanhope's translation. Yet I had frequently much sensible comfort in reading him, such as I was an utter stranger to before; and meeting likewise with a religious friend, which I had never had till now, I began to alter the whole form of my convocation, and to set in earnest upon a new life. I set apart an hour or two a day for religious retirement. I communicated [took Holy Communion] every week. I watched against all sin, whether in word or deed. I began to aim at, and pray for, inward holiness. So that now, "doing so much, living so good a life," I doubted not but I was a good Christian. [2]

John Wesley describes the rigid, legalistic, passively violent clergyman that he was as he approached the age of thirty:

In my youth I was not only a member of the Church of England [Anglican], but a bigot of it, believing none but the members of it to be in a state of salvation. . . . I began to abate of this violence in 1729. . . . But still I was as zealous as ever, observing every point of Church discipline, and teaching all my pupils so to do. . . . When I was abroad [as a missionary to America], I observed every rule of the Church, even at the peril of my life. . . . I was exactly of the sentiment when I returned from America.[3]

Finally, on the evening of May 24, 1738, at the age of thirty-four, John Wesley reports:

I went very unwillingly to a society in Aldersgate Street, where one was reading Luther's preface to the epistle to the Romans. About a quarter before nine, while he was describing the change which God works in the heart through faith in Christ, I felt my heart strangely warmed. I felt that I did trust in Christ, Christ alone for salvation; and an assurance was given me that he had taken away my sins, even mine, and saved me

---

[2]John Wesley, *The Journal of John Wesley*, A.M., ed. Nehemiah Curnock (London: Robert Culley, n.d.), 1:465–67.

[3]John Wesley, *The Letters of the Rev. John Wesley*, A.M., ed. John Telford (London: Epworth Press, 1931), 8:140.Wesley, Letters, 5:16.

from the law of sin and death. And herein I found the difference between this and my former state chiefly consisted. I was striving, yea, fighting with all my might under the law, as well as under grace. But then I was sometimes, if not often conquered; now I was always conqueror.[4]

This was not to be the end of the pilgrimage for John Wesley. His journal and private diary are dotted with further transformations, and a letter to his brother Charles on December 15, 1772, notes a low point from which he longs for the security of the legalism of his old university years: "I often cry out, 'My former happy life restore!' Let me be again an Oxford Methodist! I am often in doubt whether it would not be best for me to resume all my Oxford rules, great and small."

What had John Wesley being doing? He had been the instrument of revival and awakening on two continents. And his simple "rule" for obedience to God was to live out what he came to call "perfect love." It consisted of following two principles in which Jesus boiled down all the Law and the Prophets: "Love the Lord your God with all your heart, with all your soul, and with all your mind [and] love your neighbor as yourself" (Matt. 22:37, 39).

On other occasions, John Wesley confided to his brother Charles how even more complicated his pilgrimage of faith and belief was. At times, he was likely classically depressed. Yet his integrity, and God's holiness working in him, held him steady to the end of life.

Pilgrimage, People, and Holiness

We have summarized the John Wesley pilgrimage as an invitation to reflect on your own life journey. A marriage passes through stages, a sort of pilgrimage, and marriages that get "stuck" often collapse or become ordeals to endure. In our search for a healthy pilgrimage model for a marriage, we want you to reflect on your experience and see whether it matches the usual developmental pattern.

Most of us start out (1) *egocentric*, unable to contemplate that things might be seen in any other way than our own, (2) then we tend to move to a *legalistic* (fairness) stage, and (3) a *principled* (perspectivistic) epoch

---

[4]Ibid

eventually emerges. If as individuals we can trace that sequence as we look back, then we can better understand "where the players are" in the marriage journeys. Let's look at what might happen if both players are at about the same developmental stage.

Egocentric period and marriage: Each spouse has a personal, self-serving agenda. At its best, the relationship attempts to meet each other's personal expectations with mutually beneficial deals. "I'll scratch your back if you'll scratch mine" works well if both spouses are benefitting about equally. At its worst, a marriage at this stage is a competition in which spouse adversaries make demands, manipulate events and money, and take what they can get away with. They make threats, deny attention or affection, and engage in a series of games that keep them stuck in an infantile marriage. If even one person is stuck on egocentrism, that tends to drag the other spouse into the strategies of that stage in order to survive. So everybody loses.

Legalistic period and marriage: Here roles are clearly and rigidly defined. Talk of "my work and your work" emerges. Nobody is happy if either is unhappy. A careful balancing of responsibilities and rewards can turn this into a happy, well-calibrated home. Sit-down-and-talk sessions tend to define more and more divisions of labor and responsibility. However, the couple's concepts of "what a man is supposed to do" and "what a woman is supposed to do" often get stuck here in a common separation of powers.

Principled period and marriage: Emphasis here is on looking at the whole marriage and all responsibilities, dividing assignments to match gifts so that low energy is required. Roles are more fluid and more things are done as a team. Intimacy and communication flourish, since almost no energy is used in competition, self-protection and getting even.

Stated even more simply, a married couple tends to spend most of their time focused on issues appropriate to where they are in this life pilgrimage:

1. *Egocentric agenda:* having fun, getting what "I" want, working on getting "individual needs" met.

2. *Legalistic agenda:* defining roles, asserting rights, cooperating on common goals.

3. *Principled agenda:* growing together, celebrating achievements, planning common goals.

If we were to label how the relationship might be working at each stage, look at the journey:

1. *Egocentric Stage:* symbiotic/adversary relationship.

2. *Legalistic Stage:* traditional roles and rights relationship.

3. *Principled Stage:* "two become one," each for the other.

Robbie and I speculate that marriage is probably the primary curriculum God gives most people for accelerating the spiritual journey. Add parenting, and you've gone to "graduate school" for a course that can lead to holiness! In our own marriage, we might have gotten "stuck" in the egocentric or legalistic stage. Many people who lay this three-storied grid over their own troubled marriages report they are able to see why they collapsed. "I wonder if we might have found a 'new' marriage if we had invested the energy," one divorced spouse reflected.

We wrote the first edition of this book as we were coming up on our fortieth anniversary, July 15, 1988. We passed the fifty-third marker in July of 2001. In the following pages, we want to describe some of the bumps, which served to release us from the tendency to accept getting "stuck" in a marriage. Each of these bumps required serious, hard work.

In the typical early egocentric phase, each spouse wants to get personal satisfaction out of the marriage. Ask a group of teens, as we did not long ago, "What do you like most about being a woman?" Or, "What do you like most about being a man?" Teenage men almost unanimously reply, "Being the boss, being in charge, and having a lot of freedom to do what I want to do." You can hear the implication of owning another person, being lord over her, and yet being able to get away and do what you please. This is clearly egocentric for the male. But the teenage women's responses stopped us cold as well: "I like being a woman because I don't really have to make decisions or have a lot of responsibility. I like it that I'll have someone to take care of me." You don't have to be a trained therapist to see that both the young men and the young women are headed for serious surprises in marriage. *Symbiosis*—matching two distorted expectations together until they "fit"— may feel good for awhile. But a symbiotic marriage is headed for rude surprises, likely toward anger and tears—or worse.

One way to resolve the shattered dreams of egocentrism is to make a deal to take care of each other's needs, to divide the responsibilities, and to settle down to the fact that the initial "dream" of marriage didn't work very well. The couple may reflect on the fact that they are stuck with a lot of work in this marriage. Often there are children by the time the egocentric illusion breaks down. With jobs to hold and bills to pay, the marriage feels more like a chore, with maintenance duties and responsibilities that come around with a regular schedule. There can be a large dose of self-pity during this legalistic work phase in a marriage. Each partner may take pride in "being a good mother" or "being a good father and husband," but affection is often pretty thin. The couple may not yet have developed habits of caring gestures on arriving or departing. The pain of a marginally defective sexual relationship probably haunts them. If this grind of legal obligation does not collapse, with one spouse making a run for the irresponsibility of cultural adolescence with its expensive and fast lifestyle, it can crank along until there are teenage children to make more and more demands on the family's resources. Such a marriage is ripe for one or both of the partners to find love in the workplace—an affair that requires no maintenance tasks such as the bills, children, or dull routines at home.

When there are teen children at home, the parents have vivid reminders that they are no longer young and vibrant. Often those children remind Mom and Dad of all the dreams of young love that they once cherished. This combination of a "stuck" marriage and fading youth sets up high vulnerability for leaving the marriage and starting over with somebody else's spouse. Of course, divorce only complicates the future, virtually never simplifies it. In a major study of divorced people ten years after the divorce, they unanimously expressed the regret that they had not put as much energy into improving their marriage as they invested in the search for love outside the marriage.[5]

In this book, we have tried to tell enough of our story to encourage you to "get a new marriage" with the same spouse. Our marriage has been far from perfect, yet the stages have surely been there. Looking back, we can see that our pilgrimage of a growing marriage has paid off in every way. So in this last chapter, we want to tell you where we are today and look back at the last major transition point. We feel less certain how to describe the marriage we have today than those of the two visible previous stages. You may see things in what we report here that we do not yet see. We cannot know whether there may yet be another stage awaiting us, but we know the turf of the egocentric and the legalistic years we have traveled. We have reported in some detail on those in earlier chapters. So in this final chapter, look at

---

[5]Judith S. Wallterstein and Sandra Blakeslee, *Second Chances: Men, Women, and Children a Decade After Divorce* (New York: Houghton Mifflin, 1996).

where we are today and help us evaluate and treasure what we have and how we got here.

Robbie: From Inferiority to Confidence

I think the first day I knew something was going to change was when Don laid the checkbook on the breakfast table as he was leaving for Bloomington. He said, "Robbie, will you take care of paying the bills until I get through with this Ph.D. program? It is driving me crazy trying to keep on top of everything." I was flattered, and frankly a little eager to get my hands on the business side of the household. From the time we were married, Don had insisted that I have a signature on file at the bank. He would give me a check or let me take the checkbook whenever I needed to make a purchase alone. He was not stingy, though both of us have a frugal streak, which we think is essential if we want to be generous in giving. But now things began to change. I was good at the books, records, and accounts. I had majored in accounting in my associate degree at Central College.

When Asbury Seminary called Don to teach there and Don said he wanted to take the job, I knew we were in for another major transition. We decided that Mike and I would hold steady at Winona Lake, Indiana. I could establish minimum retirement benefits in two more years at my job, and Mike could almost finish high school by then. So Don would commute more than three hundred miles each way, each week. That would make me a "widow" for three or four days each week. If we put the Indiana house on the market and bought a house in Kentucky even more turbulence might trouble our relatively routine life.

The plot did thicken because we bought the Kentucky house. It was seventy-two years old and a ruin. Don needed his free days to hire and supervise contractors, as well as do some of the interior demolition and reconstruction himself. This meant Mike and I now were the commuters. We would drive to Wilmore, Kentucky, on Friday afternoon and return to Indiana on Sunday afternoon.

If pain is a prerequisite for genuine transformation, we had our curriculum handed to us. Within the first year Don served on the faculty, I had to deal with these kinds of things: (1) The family car overheated on a trip south, the motor caught fire, and the pistons got stuck. I had to decide on having the car towed back to Winona Lake. (2) Mike's school car developed radiator problems and lost antifreeze repeatedly. (3) The septic tank of our rural Indiana home backed up, sending toxic gas into the home. (4) On one of the return trips, I left my purse in the women's room at a fuel stop. Returning in a few minutes, I found it had been stolen, complete with all of my money and credit cards, as Mike and I traveled north into the jaws of a blizzard. (5) I picked up a virus near Christmas that, with heavy antibiotics, seriously depleted my system. I looked like a ghost when Don's entire family arrived to spend our final Christmas in the Indiana home together.

During the year, I had no choice but to become a decision maker. I had always depended on Don to take care of everything. I knew he could and would "take over" when anything needed to be done or decided. In some strange way (perhaps through spiritual atrophy on my part), I had left the praying, seeking, and waiting before God to Don. He was my priest in everything. I had no idea who served as his priest or mentor. It never occurred to me that God might lead me, or that I might be able to seek and to know God's will myself, in things large or small.

I had never bought clothes, even for myself, without Don's shopping with me. (He resisted, but I wasn't comfortable unless he was there to tell me how I looked in something. He was often generous insisting that I buy "both" dresses.) Now I found I could shop for myself. I began taking over teenage discipline and guidance with Mike. Before that year, I felt that this was Don's job and he should do it. So I had no idea I could contribute to it at all.

Having to make decisions, having to deal with the consequences of my own reasoning and choices, changed everything. Suddenly, I wasn't so nervous about offering my opinion in a faculty meeting at the school where I taught or on a church committee. I also found that I could carry on a scrappy dialogue with Don. I think he was surprised, because I was invading what had been his turf of decision making. Now that I was also thinking for myself, I was less intimidated by fears of offending someone and more committed to working for the best outcomes by straightforward and clearheaded honesty. I found that I had a good mind, that I could carry on a dialogue in the wider world.

I began to develop a critical analytical ability, and that felt good. I found I could trust my intuitive judgment and could evaluate authority structures. For years, I had been a passive, silent partner, virtually a "nonparticipating stockholder" everywhere.

I had a greatly improved sense of my own self. I was able to release my husband and sons, without loading my low self-esteem on them and binding us all with my feelings of inferiority and shame. I felt "ten feet tall," capable, competent, and a whole person before God.

After taking the Myers-Briggs personality profile, I was wonderfully affirmed to find that my gifts were vastly different from Don's. I knew I had been making positive contributions to the marriage and I was exhilarated to discover that I could be set free to make even more. I knew too that I was not having to remake Don in my own image, nor would he need to remake me into his. "Together," he once said, "we have a whole set of dominoes, but either of us alone would be operating with only a half a set." This open window on the variety of God's gifts, in creating personalities so different from each other, put me at ease around everyone. I could see how much I needed people who had seemed odd to me because they were different.

At first Don took the initiative about church attendance. We never missed a service except for illness or our complicated schedule. That meant an average of five services each week, if you count Sunday school and youth meetings in which some of us were involved during our two decades of child rearing and launching.

Don was reasonable. The boys' agendas sometimes blocked an occasional church meeting for all of us, but I never had to ask whether we would be going to church. After all, Don was an ordained minister, whether serving as a pastor or as a denominational executive. It was his business to support the church, so I accepted all of that without thinking, without discussion. The boys did, as well. None of us realized that perhaps we were "going through the motions," which were not putting all of us in touch with what the real issues of worship and community are.

Then, when Don was gone on Wednesday night, I had to decide whether to go to midweek prayer meeting. So I quit going for a while as things got more and more complicated. Don always got us around and off to church. But when our problems began to stack up, I turned to God for myself. I began studying the Bible on a very systematic basis and got a new vision of who God is. This brought worship services and prayer meetings into an important new personal focus for me.

I also established my daily "quiet time" as a rigorous priority—out of desperation! Today, that time has expanded substantially and includes an early morning prayer partner once each week, with a special intercessory dimension to our conversations and praying.

I sensed that our marriage was changing. I no longer watched Don so closely or worried that he might offend someone in his work as a national leader in the church. That changed my side of the relationship. I now felt like a true partner and peer. I found myself willing to "set him free" to be his own person. I think my sense of respect for him established a new level of trust and freedom for both of us. While I was never a smothering or jealous wife, I did "mother" Don a lot and worry about his hurting his reputation by saying or doing something stupid. When I saw that I wasn't responsible for Don's actions I was no longer nervous that he might offend someone. I suddenly "let him go," knowing that if he got his foot in his mouth, he could get it out. We both became adults in some amazing and deeply satisfying ways.

The last twenty-five years, however, have provided a unique crucible for growth and transformation. In almost any week, we encounter challenges that require investing new energy in meeting needs of our extending family and the widening circle of seminary graduates who continue to visit us. We have laid all four of our parents in the hands of God, welcomed three great-grandsons to the family circle, and celebrated the fact that the four generations of our immediate family are literally in a close circle, including us in much of their lives. We have learned better how to "weep with those who weep"and "rejoice with those who rejoice" (Rom. 12:15).

I am a woman at peace with myself. I have retired from teaching school after more than thirty-nine years in the classroom. Don and I look after great-grandsons Tyler, Caleb, and Isaiah, sometimes having all three of them in our home for most of a day while their parents are at school or work. We are the story masters for them. Don is their movie accomplice as he joins them to watch The Bear *or* The Grinch That Stole Christmas. *Don and I are a tremendous team, handling the many challenges that face us. We celebrate the long and grand years we have had, and we are delighting in the journey—whatever comes to us.*

Don: From Control to Empowering

As I try to retrace the pattern in our marriage, I confess that on our wedding day when I was about to turn twenty years old, I thought largely in egocentric terms. My view of marriage was that I was "taking a wife." She was a "showpiece," and many of the accessories of the marriage tradition seem to emphasize the idea of "bride as property." All of this was made secure by a legal document that, while it conveyed no wealth to me, did seem to convey this woman to me and actually renamed her as mine in a tangible way.

I do not want to suggest that I began to abuse Robbie or treat her as a slave. But I did have heavy expectations of services she would render, of areas of labor that were to be hers, and of a long-term obligation to bear my children. In our better times I was a benevolent monarch. I was kind to her. I was a wise lover who tempered my desires to stay within the limits of her interests. Yet I made commitments that required her to perform. I brought guests home unannounced for meals or overnight stays. I was baffled when, in the presence of witnesses (especially of my family), she would tell anecdotes that put me in a bad light. Clearly, my private exploitation of her was being recounted in these conversations to hurt me. My dictatorship was evoking some resentment. Most of the time, her resentments were not visible; but now and then she would make me squirm into compliance by using a little blackmail.

A little before age thirty-five, I gave up on having it my way. I still had my own ideal of marriage, but I could see that, while some marriages might be well synchronized and "everybody got what they wanted," I was never going to have what I wanted in my marriage. I occasionally ventilated my frustration to Robbie. In these episodes, I exposed some streaks of self-pity at having to relinquish my petty wishes. I sensed that things were never going to change, so I retaliated. The legalistic/silent truce era consisted of a freeze-out game: If I can't have what I want, you won't get what you want either.

I kept up my end of the family responsibility, but no more. Our roles were well-established, almost fenced apart. Now and then, we openly blamed each other when outside responsibilities took either of us away from "doing our job" at home. We usually maintained this orderly household through duty and habit, but monitored it with occasional nagging, even shouting exchanges that evoked enough guilt to whip each other back into line.

Robbie and I had mostly good days. We had a good, functional marriage. We looked good in public, especially at church, where we were conspicuously visible as a family on a front pew. But we both knew ours was not a rich and ripening marriage. We were consumed by parenting tasks. We were fanatical about supporting our sons in their school, music, church, and athletic events—of which there were many. We were also consumed by our volunteer work with the youth in our large church. I directed as many as six choirs every week, including the sanctuary choir with platform responsibility for congregational singing. Besides these occupations, our professional careers were advancing, claiming increasing blocks of time beyond the workday.

This vocational expansion eventually forced us to enter the third major epoch, where we continue to grow. I became immersed in doctoral studies at Indiana University. Robbie simultaneously began graduate work on a reading specialist's certificate. My program required a one-year technical residency. I was able to enroll for a full load to satisfy that requirement, and commuted from two hundred miles away. On the day I gave the checkbook to Robbie, my armor cracked. I had literally carried the checkbook because I felt that was uniquely a masculine task. It never occurred to me to ask Robbie to do anything financial. I was stereotyped into an absolute conformity to a role pattern I had adopted from the culture around me.

Even though Robbie had an accounting and bookkeeping major in her junior-college degree, I had never even considered asking her to manage any of our financial affairs. I bought cars, obligated our income, purchased furniture, and ordered equipment without so much as reporting to her what I was doing.

When I cried out to Robbie for help, I still remember that she took the checkbook and responded with a quiet, "Okay." Immediately, our financial life came into order. Our checkbook and the monthly ledger sheets from the bank suddenly came into balance for the first time in our married lives. I have never carried the checkbook since then. That was in 1968, as I was turning forty.

In February of 1971, I began two and a half years of commuting each week from Winona Lake, Indiana, to Wilmore, Kentucky. This set up the period of stress that Robbie reported. But there were astonishing and completely unpredictable benefits. I found my fondness and admiration for Robbie were energized by the four days we were apart each week. I slept in a single bed in my temporary guest quarters on campus, then later in our mansion under renovation. Some nights, I never even turned over. I could crawl out of bed in the morning with only a minor adjustment necessary to leave it perfectly made up. In our habituated nocturnal intimacy at home, we rolled, embraced, turned, and reembraced a dozen times or more each night, in what must have been very light fits of sleep. Now we had new experiences to report to each other from our separate worlds. We were starved to see each other. Our affection seemed alive and fresh. We were more sexually charged than we had been in fifteen years. It was clear we had a new marriage.

I took enormous pleasure in the excellent decisions Robbie was making. *I am married to an excellent manager*, I remember thinking. I hope I said it to her at the time. She is so effective in supervision that whenever we need a contractor for home repairs today, we look at the options now open to us and most often we agree that Robbie will supervise the work. Both of us can get executive work done, though we use quite different paths to completion.

It gradually became clear to me that this reticent women, whom God has so wisely brought in to my life, was showing signs of becoming a spiritual giant. In addition, I was pleased that she was being pulled into important public school and church responsibilities. Within a few years of her move to Kentucky, she was elected president of the Jessamine County Teachers Association and repeatedly represented school concerns to the state legislature. I was occasionally her consort at official banquets where she handled the lectern, made the speeches, and was the visible leader in her domain.

Today, we have a marriage that is characterized by a rock-solid base of mutual respect and skillful attention to the care of each other. If I am ill, Robbie sees the symptoms before I am even aware the fever is rising. When she comes down with a virus, I get absolutely aggressive and see to it that she gets medical attention. There are a thousand tasks that were once "sex-typed," but that we now share or switch in order to distribute the time or energy investment of our lives. It is clear to me that Robbie will make a good and healthy widow, should that ever become her challenge. She is a complete woman. I can read Proverbs 31 to her in celebration. I could even add a few stanzas to enlarge on Robbie's unique competencies. When our accountant phones, he always asks to speak to Robbie. They understand each other. And I am glad.

A Three-Stage Marriage Trajectory?

We cannot say whether every marriage must pass through the egocentric and legalistic stages. We are simply reporting the stages we can see in general human development and the clear marks they have in the history of our own marriage. If we had never been "stressed" into the crises that pushed us into the principled level, we think we could never have seen the structure of those early and middle years. Maybe you cannot draw a map until you have driven blindly over the road.

Stage one—egocentric lovers are likely to be so involved in the "game of loving" that there is little concern to figure out what is happening to other folks. Most young lovers watch their parents and wonder whatever happened to their love and affection. Many of them cannot imagine their parents' enjoying anything resembling "making out" or "having sex." The young tend to give up on making sense out of the older generation anyway, and they attribute other marital patterns to the "olden days." The egocentric lovers are so absorbed with getting the thrill of marriage that, so long as they can work out a reciprocal, mutually satisfying relationship, they are indifferent to how anyone else lives. Indeed, some of them refuse to marry because they see their married friends moving into conflict and treating each other badly.

Stage two—legalistic lovers are negotiating a functional marriage, meeting payments, shuttling kids to school, feeling the drudgery of being a parent and a spouse. The marriage manuals and marriage seminars abound to "define the roles" for this stage of marriage, equipping husband and wife to be even more functional than before. The leaders of most of these seminars coach people on getting things right. Couples in this legal stage are vulnerable to such teaching. It calls for them to turn up the heat on gender-defined roles, to study them, and to pay attention to the authority statements that the seminar leaders offer. They codify everything, cite chapter and verse, and list the rules in numbered order. The major output of marriage manuals and so-called biblical models for the family comes from people with this penchant for legalistic rules, regulations, authority, and conflict management.

Stage three—principle-driven lovers have set each other free and have laid down their lives and energies to exalt each other. Only they are able to look at the young, playful, egocentric crowd and celebrate their innocent games, knowing that God can lead them to richer, less-manipulative agendas farther up the road. Principled lovers are also able to match up their own power-and-conflict history with the popular models that stress roles and rules. These mellower couples know that some of the people who follow those patterns will also break free to love one another without fear and without preoccupation for announcing their own status and security needs.

In this chapter we have opened the most recent transformation of our marriage in a way that we have not previously discussed outside our own home. We have been grateful that, across the years, we have had three good marriages—each of them quite different, but all of them to each other! All of them have been characterized by fidelity, affection, and unquestioned commitment to see each other "till death do us part." No doubt, at any moment along the pilgrimage of our three visible marriages, we would have claimed the present as the best. Even now, however, we expect that the best is yet to be.

If we have offended you by the thesis of this book, by all means get on with your own marriage. Lay this book aside. Feel anger or even pity for us. Take your marriage to Scripture and hammer out your own manual of procedures. But if you ever feel that your marriage is "getting you down," pick up this copy of *Two Become One* and see whether there are helpful coaching tips for you then. We salute you, and we leave you and your honest search in the hands of God.

Questions People Ask

Q. *Do you mean to suggest that it is inevitable that young lovers will have to go through all of the stages you have found? Why couldn't they start out where you finished?*

A. We believe they can. In fact, we think we have seen that phenomenon. Couples who work through the FOCCUS Inventory with a mentoring couple, beginning before their wedding and continuing well into the early years of marriage, are far ahead of couples who do not have that set of resources.[6] Couples who avoid marriage until they have invested in egocentric dating (even living-together experiments) run the risk of becoming more and more self-protective, often permanently locked into egocentrism. How any couple moves through the challenges of marriage is their own choice, and every marriage is unique. We want to encourage everyone to keep welcoming painful opportunity and to see it as a door to a potential new marriage with the same spouse.

---

[6]The couple inventory developed by FOCCUS, Inc., Family Life Offices, 3214 North Sixtieth Street, Omaha, Nebraska 68104 (phone 402-551-9003), is designed for use by a mentor couple with premarriage preparation, following through the first year of marriage. The six categories provide couple responses for dialogue and exploration under mentor supervision. Where entire communities have adopted FOCCUS as premarriage preparation, the divorce rate has dropped by as much as 35 percent in five years. For couples ready for postmarriage evaluation, the REFOCCUS instrument is available in a self-scoring version for mentored exploration of the same crucial issues in marriage.

Subject Index

Scripture Reference Index

Books on Marriage
and Family Relationships
from Donald & Robbie Joy . . .

Donald M. Joy is Director of the Center for the Study of the Family in Wilmore, Kentucky, and an adjunct professor at Asbury Theological Seminary. He and his wife, Robbie B. Joy, lead Christian marriage enrichment seminars throughout the United States.

Evangel Publishing House is pleased to recommend these books for your family library. . . .

Empower Your Kids To Be Adults

Teenagers in Western culture have grown up in a society that tries to build their self-esteem and encourages them to "leave their options open." As a result, many adolescents are not prepared to deal with adult life.

Dr. Joy explains how adults can model mature relationships that help young people grow up. He challenges adults to lead young people into a responsible pattern of life, so they can begin to make mature decisions.

152 Pages 6"x9" Paperback
ISBN 1-928915-01-9 $12.95

Bonding: Relationships in the Image of God

When God made us to desire relationships with others, just as He does. In this challenging book, discover . . .

❏ *"Pair bonding" as part of God's design for all human beings*

❏ *The lifetime effects of "birth bonding"*

❏ *"Family bonding" as the anchor for children's sex roles and identities*

160 Pages 6"x9" Paperback
ISBN 0-916035-69-7 $12.95

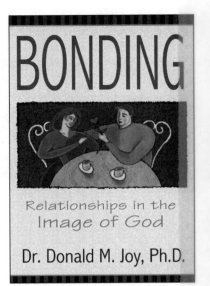

Re-Bonding: Preventing and Restoring Damaged Relationships

We live in a society that discourages long-term intimate relationships. Promiscuity and "do-as-you-please" morality have severed the cords uniting parent with child, husband with wife, and friend with friend.

Dr. Joy warns of the pain that follows casual intimacy, but holds out the hope of restoring relationships that have been carelessly wrecked in this way. Scripture points the way to a new life beyond premarital sex, adultery, and rebellion.

144 Pages 6"x9" Paperback
ISBN 0-916035-70-0 $12.95

Men Under Construction: Rebuilding the Way to Healthy Sexuality, Relationships, and Identity

First published in 1988, before the Christian men's movement became popular, this book first drew attention to men's need for vital support groups. Now revised and expanded, *Men Under Construction* is an essential tool for leaders of men's groups.

Former Dallas Cowboys coach Tom Landry noted that *Men Under Construction* "offers a well-thought-out game plan that will help you" become a man after God's own heart.

190 Pages 5-1/2"x8-1/2" Paperback
ISBN 1-56476-053-7 $12.95

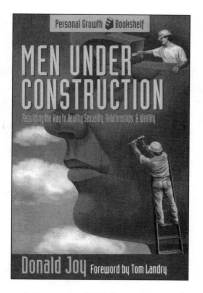

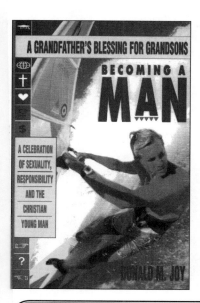

Becoming a Man: A Celebration of Sexuality, Responsibility, and the Christian Young Man

Dr. Joy offers insightful, caring wisdom on the topics every young man will face, including:

❏ **The physical and emotional changes of becoming a man**

❏ **Dreaming of the future and making those dreams come true**

❏ **Relationships with girls and when to get serious**

128 Pages 5-1/2"x8-1/2" Paperback
ISBN 1-56476-053-7 $12.95

Available at your local bookstore or call
Evangel Publishing House
(800) 253-9315
www.evangelpublishing.com

Two Become One: God's Blueprint for Couples

After more than fifty years of marriage, the Joys share their insights into what the Bible says about authority and responsibility in Christian marriage. They reexamine biblical texts that are often used to justify "keeping women silent" in the church and giving men full responsibility for decision-making in the home.

This practical and sometimes controversial book deserves careful study by Christian couples and those who counsel them.

192 Pages 6"x9" Paperback
ISBN 1-928915-27-2 $14.95